Fun Food Facts

Mike Bellino

authorHOUSE®

AuthorHouse™
1663 Liberty Drive, Suite 200
Bloomington, IN 47403
www.authorhouse.com
Phone: 1-800-839-8640

Illustrations by Christopher M. Bellino.

First published by AuthorHouse 9/24/2008

ISBN: 978-1-4343-7770-8 (sc)

Library of Congress Control Number: 2008908808

Printed in the United States of America
Bloomington, Indiana

This book is printed on acid-free paper.

Dedication

I dedicate this book to my Mom, who taught me to cook, and my Dad who is my chief editor. I also dedicate this to my wife, Mary, who has been a terrific help and support for this book; one project in a long chain of crazy projects I've engaged in over the years. Finally, I must give thanks to God for the yearning to understand His creation.

Table of Contents

Foreword ix

Author's Response to the Foreword x

Introduction xi

How did cooking get started? 1

Milk: Good food for a good long time 2

Butter (and margarine) 6

Cheese 9

Yogurt 13

Fruits 15

Vegetables 21

Mushrooms 30

Starch 32

Bread 33

Meet Meat 36

Herbs & Spices 44

Coffee 47

Chocolate 52

Onion & Garlic 56

The Cereals 59

    Corn *64*

Wine and Beer 70

Sweet Stuff… 75

    Honey *75*

    Sugar *77*

Substitute sugar 82
Ice Cream.. 83

Vitamins 86

Tidbits & Morsels 89

Bibliography - Recommended Reading.............................. 101

Index 105

Foreword

In the spirit of the earliest humans, Mike has always been a "hunter-gatherer" of one sort or another. As a small child walking to school, he would gather a plant, insect, stone, or shell. Each day his classmates would eagerly greet him wondering what he would bring to show them and to hear his rendition of the "facts".

His paternal grandmother referred to him as a "mix-master". For those who don't know, that was the "Kitchen Aide Mixer" of the nineteen-sixties. Kitchen Aide was not available in the mass market back then. He was always into everything, wondering what he could disassemble, get a chemical reaction from, or how to develop a better recipe. He tried everything from made home-made volcanoes, fireworks and go-carts, the likes of which you'll never see. His current hobby is model rocketry. On any given day you might find him, when not at his full time job in engineering, raising his own pigs, chickens for eggs (his kids gather the eggs), foraging for berries, making maple syrup, gardening and raising honey bees on his Circle Bell farm in New Hampshire. Those hunter-gathering genes are alive and well!

As a youngster a favorite treat was his "wacky cake". Every Friday after school he made one, much to the delight of his siblings. It is a cake mixed in the pan you bake it in, and actually was quite tasty. He loved to make sausage for holiday celebrations. That was his job -- grinding the meat, adding spices and herbs and stuffing into casings. While growing up, he learned to make bread, pizza, pancakes, and a family favorite; ox-eye eggs. He was the matzo maker for Passover too.

He was generally interested in cooking while developing a keen interest in spices and herbs. While preparing meals he uses an array of spices and herbs. Used properly, spices and herbs make for delicious, interesting, and healthy food! At family gatherings, many of our conversations center on food, herbs, and spices: where to find them, how to use and store them and then experimenting to see what pleases the palate.

In so many ways, it seems natural for him to write this book on Fun Food Facts.

Having been inspired as a child by Laura Ingalls Wilder books, he is now a country boy, who enjoys where he lives and what he does. What will he jump into next? Only tomorrow will tell. In the meantime, enjoy "Fun Food Facts"!

"The more things that thou learnest to know and enjoy, the more complete and full will be for thee the delight of living" - August Graf von Platen

That sums up Mike.

- Joanne G. "Mom" Bellino

Author's Response to the Foreword

Aw shucks, Mom!

Introduction

"In what art or science other than cooking could improvements be made that would more powerfully contribute to increase the comforts and enjoyments of mankind?"

– Sir Benjamin Thompson,
Count Rumford

So why Fun Food Facts? If you're curious and like concise facts, as I do, then Fun Food Facts is for you! If you are like me, you ask many questions about the whys and hows of cooking. As I look for answers, I've noticed a variety of books and web sites I have read tend to be either dry or indirect in their presentation of food facts. Why not present the facts in a way that is brief, informative and fun? It will likely improve your cooking skills as your knowledge of the various foods and cooking facts broadens. You will find this book a handy reference that you will want to keep in the kitchen.

It is my hope that this book will help people to learn and be motivated to learn more. I believe the Fun Food Facts will make cooking more interesting and encourage creativity. I am certain that Fun Food Facts will improve your culinary skills as it has mine. If nothing else, it will make you a small-talk star at the next party!

If you would like to contact me regarding questions, comments or corrections send e-mail to: FunFoodFacts@yahoo.com. I will make every effort to respond to all correspondence. I look forward to hearing from you!

How did cooking get started?

Anthropologists believe that humans began cooking at least 250,000 years ago. Probably a fire started by lightning baked exposed tubers (edible roots such as potato, carrot, yam). These tubers would have been easier to eat and tasted better. Eventually fire was contained into cooking pits and similar gastronomical benefits were discovered for cooking raw meat.

From a survival perspective, cooking food made it easier to eat, digest and rendered plant poisons innocuous. It is also believed that the daily pattern of bringing food back to the fire pit may have helped in the formation of pair bonding and families.

Milk:
Good food for a good
long time

I occasionally wonder how silly the first human may have felt approaching a cow, or some other lactating beast, and squirting the white liquid into their mouth or bowl. We will never know how silly that human may have felt but a satisfied belly would have been the result.

Milk is a universal food that is quite nearly a complete meal – it contains water, proteins, fat, vitamins and milk sugar (lactose). Its good taste and terrific nutrition has engrained milk in many cultures, religions and philosophies.

When did milking animals begin?
Records of humans milking animals dates back as far as 6,000 years ago. Fresh milk, butter and cheese became popular in Egypt, Northern Europe and Asia.

How about milk in the Mediterranean?
Despite today's universal appeal, milk was not universally accepted. The Greeks and Romans thought anyone who drank milk was a barbarian, as that is what the barbarians did and they didn't. The phrase "milk drinker" (galaktopotes) was a derogatory name the Greeks cast in reference to the barbarians. The Greeks/Romans did not drink milk, it is theorized, because the climate was too warm for storage. Cheese, on the other hand, was quite popular in the Mediterranean region.

Does milk make the skin more supple?
I will place the burden of proof on the cosmetics experts. However, the wife of Domitius Nero, Poppea, would take her baths in milk believing this would help her complexion. When she took her show on the road, she'd bring 500 nursing donkeys along to ensure an ample supply of "bathwater".

What does "Homogenized" in milk production mean?
Homogenization (derived from the Greek "of the same kind") involves forcing the milk through a high pressure nozzle onto a hard surface. This breaks up the larger milk fat globules into smaller ones such that they cannot rise to the top and form a cream layer. If this was not done, we would have to constantly shake or stir our milk to keep the taste and consistency of our glass of milk the same.

What is the difference between whole, skim and low-fat milk?
It's often thought that skim milk or 2% has a great deal less fat than whole milk. In fact, whole milk is 4% milk fat, low-fat is 2% milk fat, skim milk is 0.1% milk fat. 2% milk, for example, does not mean that 98% of the fat has been removed; it means that the percentage of milk fat present in milk has been reduced from 4% to 2%.

What does "Pasteurization" in milk processing mean?
The old joke says that if you leave a cow too long in the pasture, it becomes pasteurized. In actual fact, it was the French scientist, Louis Pasteur, who in the 1860's, invented heat treatments for wine and beer. This process killed off disease-causing bacteria. In the 1940's various US states began to require Pasteurization of milk that not only made the milk safer to drink but extended the shelf life as well.

The standard Pasteurization process involves heating the milk to 144ºF (62ºC) for 30 minutes. Optionally, the milk may be heated quickly to 160°F (71°C) for 15 seconds. The latter method requires more process control and risks affecting flavor.

What is "Lactose Intolerant"?

The milk sugar, lactose, is only present in cow's milk. From infancy to about 3 ½ years old, the typical human body creates lactase (an enzyme) that can breakdown the lactose for digestion. The races from Northern Europe tend to keep producing lactase into adulthood but other races, such as from Africa and Asia, do not. When the body cannot break down the lactose, then it is said to be lactose intolerant.

How is it that lactose intolerance causes discomfort?

If Lactose is not broken down by Lactase, the Lactose passes into the colon and is digested by various bacteria. When the bacteria digest the lactose, they create the by-product of carbon dioxide gas. It is this gas production which can make us feel bloated and uncomfortable. The difference in our reaction to lactose can depend on the types and amount of bacteria present in our intestines.

Does light affect milk?

Sunlight can disrupt the milk molecular chains even if kept cold. Too much light imparts a burnt flavor in the milk and destroys the vitamin riboflavin.

In cooking, what does the term "scalded milk" mean?

Scalding milk involves heating the milk at 198°F (92°C) for 1 minute or 185°F (85°C) for 7 minutes. The easiest way to scald milk is to slowly heat the milk in a sauce pan over low heat. Do not allow the milk to boil! When the milk has a distinct surface "skin" over most of the area, it is scalded. Remove immediately from the heat and allow to cool.

Scalding milk alters its serum proteins in a manner such that they will not react with flour proteins, avoiding a slack bread dough. The benefits are higher rising dough and lighter bread. Scalding is also beneficial for making yogurt. Be sure to allow the scalded milk to cool to at least 105ºF (41ºC) otherwise the hot milk will kill the yeast.

Can I use whipping cream for heavy cream?
Whipping cream has about 5% less milk fat than heavy cream. You can use one for the other but the heavy cream, with its higher fat content, will whip up faster and firmer than whipping cream.

Which is heavier- one cup of Heavy Cream or one cup of Light Cream?
Heavy cream is lighter because it contains more fat (in the form of cream) and fat is less dense than water. You have my permission to win a few bets with this Fun Food Fact!

Butter (and margarine)

How is butter made?
Cream is skimmed off cow's milk and churned until it coalesces into clumps of butter in a liquid. The cream's small butterfat globules are isolated from each other by protein membranes. The churning breaks down the membranes and allows the butterfat to combine. In the old days, the cream was soured (allowed to stand for a day or two) in order to reduce the churning time. Today, machines can churn the cream into butter even when the cream is fresh. Fresh cream yields sweet butter. When the lumps of butter are formed, the liquid (buttermilk, see below) is washed out (or else it will turn the butter rancid) and the butter remains.

What is buttermilk?
Buttermilk is the liquid that is the by-product of making butter. Buttermilk is sometimes fermented to increase its acid content and improve flavor. Because it has a higher acid content, it reacts with baking soda to make more carbon dioxide gas that, for example, results in fluffy pancakes and biscuits.

Why is salt added to butter?

Salt is added as a preservative. With refrigeration today, salt is not needed for preservation; however we have grown accustomed to the flavor. It is best to use unsalted butter when called for in a recipe, but if you must use salted butter, reduce or eliminate any additional salt.

My recipe calls for buttermilk but I don't have any on hand?

Put 1 tablespoon of white vinegar or lemon juice into a measuring cup. Add enough milk to make 1 cup total. Let the milk sit for 5 minutes.

What is clarified butter?

Butter normally contains proteins and salts. To clarify butter, heat the butter until just melted. Skim off the froth (whey proteins) and then pour off (separate) the clear butter leaving the white sediment behind. Cooking with clarified butter allows for higher temperatures and leaves a more delicate taste.

What is "ghee"?

Ghee, from traditional Indian cooking, is clarified butter but before separating, the solids are browned. This imparts a slightly nutty flavor to the butter.

What is "European" butter?

Sometime called "dry" butter, European butter is made by squeezing out several percent more buttermilk from the butter than other butters. The result is a higher percentage of butterfat, more flavor and a creamier texture.

What sort of cow does margarine come from?

Margarine is actually a spread made from vegetable oils (which is to say, it does not come from a cow). The name comes from the Greek word "*margaron*" meaning "pearl" due to the pearl shaped solids observed in the initial research. Margarine is less expensive than butter, has no cholesterol and may have less saturated fats (depending on the type of oil or hydrogenation used).

The introduction of margarine to consumers in the 1880s was resisted heavily by politicians and the dairy industry. In some states, margarine was not allowed to be yellow, was heavily taxed and labeled as a harmful drug in an effort to dissuade consumers from purchasing it. In one case, it was not until 1967 that margarine could be sold in Wisconsin. Today, given lower costs and perceived health benefits, we consume several times more margarine than butter.

Cheese

When did cheese making start?
Egyptian tombs from as far back as 4,300 years ago reveal remains of cheese. It amazed early humans that out of a liquid (milk) would come a solid (cheese). This fact eventually took on a religious meaning as it seemed to them to explain how the earth was created -- that is, out of "nothingness" came solid earth. The vestiges of this notion still exists in our language as the Greek word for milk (gala) is found in words like "galaxy" and "galaxis" ("milky way").

How is cheese made?
Cheese is the product of a chemical reaction between the milk protein casein (which becomes curds) and Rennet. Rennet is found in the 4th stomach of a milk-fed calf but is also available from other natural and man-made sources. Natural rennet is extremely efficient as it can cause the protein to coagulate (i.e. lump together) even at one part rennet in 5 million parts of milk.

After coagulation, the watery whey is pressed out of the curds (which may be used for whey cheeses such as ricotta and mysost). The now dense curds are cut into blocks and ripened. The ripening is basically the onset of mold and bacteria in a controlled (cave-like) environment -- 50 deg F at 80% RH (Relative Humidity) (hard cheese) or 95% RH (soft cheese). The cool temperature keeps the growths slow and steady. The humidity keeps the cheeses from drying out. As the bacteria or molds spread, they transform the cheese texture, composition and hence, taste.

The cheese process was most probably accidentally discovered by someone in pre-historic times who used an animal's stomach for storing milk. They soon learned that the lumps of cheese curds that formed from the milk could be formed into cheese. As the process was passed around civilization, the variations in temperature, humidity and molds gave rise to various cheeses.

Is there a connection between cottage cheese and cottages?
Cottage cheese does not require fermenting in special rooms or caves so it could be made wherever the milk supply is collected. Cottage cheese was so named because it was principally made at farmhouse cottages. It is made from the buttermilk leftover from churning butter. The cottage cheese is separated from the buttermilk using either rennet or lactic acid. Once the curds are firm enough, the liquid whey is drained off.

Why does cheese stink?
The French have long noted some people have an aversion to cheese and its powerful aroma and taste. Indeed the mold/bacteria by-products of cheese ripening includes the aromatic fragrances of lactic acid and ammonia. Cheeses such as Brie, Limburger and Camembert have higher levels of ammonia than most cheeses. As for Camembert, this cheese has earned a French Poet's title "les pieds de Dieu". Translation: The feet of God.

How do the holes in Swiss cheese get there?
The starter bacteria of Swiss cheese includes certain bacteria (*Propionibacter shermanii*) which consumes the lactic acid excreted

by the other bacteria. The by-product of this consumption is copious amounts of carbon dioxide which collects in large pockets (or "eyes") creating the Swiss cheese holes.

Is there a difference between orange and white cheddar cheese?
Other than color, no. Cheddar cheese is traditionally white but sometimes coloring is added to please personal preferences. This preference stems from the fact that milk cows produce better milk when fresh grass is plentiful and the milk, due to higher levels of beta-carotene (the orange pigment in carrots), has a yellowish tint to it. To make lesser milk look good, orange color was added with beta-carotene or annatto (seed from a tropical tree). This habit carried over into cheese-making and thus we have orange cheddar cheese.

Why do foreign cheeses taste better then American cheeses?
In America, the USDA requires all milk to be pasteurized before being turned into cheese. This eliminates nearly all bacteria in the cheese other than the active cultures added by the cheese maker. The USDA claims this is for safety, but as for taste, the extraneous cultures in unpasteurized milk adds character to the flavor. The so-called raw-milk cheese (including imports) are required by law to be aged at least 60 days.

Cheese can prevent cavities?
Mold-ripened cheeses like Roquefort have the bacteria fighting Penicillin and it has been shown to also retard the growth of teeth-eating Streptococci bacteria. So, as culinary author Brillat-Savarin penned a hundred years ago, "a dinner which ends without cheese is like a beautiful woman with only one eye", serve cheese at the end of the meal. It satisfies the palette and helps preserve the teeth.

What is Spider Cheese?
Spider cheese is more properly named Milbenkäse (mite cheese).

Mike Bellino

This cheese is made in the village of Würchwitz, Germany. In a tradition dating back to the Middle Ages, the cheese is formed into small balls and set to age in wooden boxes infested with mites. The mites burrow into the cheese rind. The mites are fed rye flour, and over time, their excrement causes fermentation to occur in the cheese. The cheese is aged from three months to a year. When the cheese is served, it is served up in its entirety: cheese, rind, excrement and live mites. Don't even think of offering a slice of Spider Cheese to little Miss Muffet!

Yogurt

Yogurt's recent history

Yogurt is a food of the ancients but relatively new to America where it has only caught on in the last 40 years. Yogurt is a bacterial culture (Lactobacillus bulgarius and Streptococcus thermophilus) grown in milk. The bacteria feed off of the lactose (milk sugar). As the bacteria grows, it produces lactic acid which creates the bitter taste of plain yogurt.

The first commercial yogurt produced, after a change of hands, was named Danone after the Spanish founder's son, Daniel. Eventually renamed Dannon, the yogurt company added fruit to offset the tart lactic acid as a novelty which met with great success.

Is Yogurt healthy?

Yes, Yogurt is high in protein, calcium and potassium. There are claims that some yogurt cultures can survive the strong stomach acid and make it to the intestines where it aides digestion. There is conflicting research on this matter and it may depend largely on the type of culture and if a beneficial quantity survives.

Can I make yogurt at home?

Yes, and it's quite easy to make, much cheaper than store bought and tastes better than the commercial yogurt.

Yogurt starts with milk (whole, part skim or skim) and a live yogurt culture. For the culture, buy a small container of any plain yogurt that contains an active yogurt culture. Put 6 cups of milk in a sauce pan on the stove. Heat over medium heat, stirring occasionally.

Milk must be first heated to about 195 deg F in order to break down the milk proteins (see scalding milk). If not scalded, the yogurt will come out as large course clumps. Use a candy thermometer to gauge the temperature, but one can also look for a thin film which forms at the top of the milk to indicate the milk has been scalded. Do not allow the milk to boil!

Turn off the heat and allow it to cool down to 120 deg F. Now stir in 3-4 tablespoons of yogurt culture. Mix well. Pour the mixture into clean glass jars. (You must use glass because the acid will interact with metal.) Cover the jars (not air tight) and put the jars into an area kept at 110 deg F for at least 4 hours. There are yogurt makers on the market which serve this purpose. Also, a warm oven will work. You can use lower temperatures but it will take longer to firm up. After your yogurt is done, store it in the refrigerator. Even at refrigerator temperatures, the bacteria will slowly continue to grow and you will notice a more tart taste as the days pass. The yogurt can stay in the fridge for about a week. Save a little yogurt to make another batch.

Fruits

How did fruit get it name?
The name derives from the Latin word "*frui*" which means to enjoy or delight in.

What is a fruit?
A fruit is defined as a plant's organ, formed from the flower, into an edible layer surrounding the seed(s). We know fruits to be apples, oranges, bananas, however by this definition, cucumbers, eggplant and tomatoes are all fruits although we call these vegetables today. A few fruits do not quite fit this definition such as the strawberry which has its seeds on the outside.

How does the fruit form?
Most fruits form after fertilization by rapid cell division at the base of the flower. Some fruits, such as the banana and navel orange do not require fertilization to form.

The final cell count is set at this first stage of development and continues to grow not in numbers but rather in size by storing water and nutrients. The watermelon, for example, expands its cell size by a factor of 350,000.

What happens when fruit ripens?
What stimulates ripening varies from fruit to fruit however in most cases the skin color changes, the flesh softens and the starches are converted to sugar. The banana, for example, converts its 25% starch content into 20% sugar content.

Some fruits can be stimulated to ripen by removing from the tree. The pear, for example, should be removed a little on the green side or it will become mealy. On the other hand, pineapples, citrus and melons do not get sweeter after picking although their texture softens somewhat.

One interesting fact is that fruit ripening is accelerated by the hydrocarbon gas, ethylene. Around 1910, it was observed that bananas placed near oranges or a burning kerosene lamp, ripened faster. It turns out that both burning kerosene and oranges emit ethylene. The ethylene causes an "autostimulation" of the fruit's ripening process. Many fruits (and tomatoes) we see in stores today were picked unripe and ripened using ethylene gas.

Figs may be ripened by "oleification" – which is applying oil to unripe figs. Long fatty-acid chains in the oil stimulates the figs to produce ethylene.

Of figs and sycophants…
During the days of the Greek empire, for reasons unknown, it was popular to smuggle figs. It is believed that people who pointed out fig smugglers to the authorities, perhaps looking for the authority's favor, were labeled as a "sycophant" which is Greek for "one who shows the fig".

How can I stop sliced bananas and apples from turning brown?
Dribble a little lemon juice over the freshly cut fruit. The acid in the lemon juice slows the enzymes, which cause the fruit to brown. If the lemon juice makes the fruit too bitter (usually it doesn't) sprinkle a little sugar over the top and mix it in.

What is the best way to store fruit?
Do not store fruit in the refrigerator. The temperature is cold enough to cause cell damage. For optimal storage, keep all fruits at 50°F (7°C). It is better to keep fruit in a cool area of the house, even if above 50°F (7°C), rather than in a refrigerator.

Why do I need to use pectin when making jam or jelly?
Pectin is a long molecule that bonds together (when properly balanced by acid and sugar) to form a mesh which holds fruit's juice. It is very difficult to achieve this "gel" and it takes a great deal of experience to get the balance of pectin, acid and sugar just right. Fruits such as strawberries, apricots and peaches require pectin to gel but grapes and most berries contain enough pectin naturally. When you purchase powdered pectin at the market, it is extracted from apples.

How many types of apples and pears are there?
Apples and pears can be found in over 7,000 varieties world wide. However, only about 100 varieties are grown commercially. The apple is more popular than the pear probably because it stores longer and does not bruise as easily. Pears are better when picked just before ripening while apples (particularly sweet apples) are best when tree ripened. If you are looking to get vitamin C from apples or pears, you had better eat them with their skin.

What is the difference between apple juice and apple cider?
Apple cider and apple juice are the same thing. However, many

manufacturers use a process to clarify the juice yielding clear apple juice. It also depends where you live on what cider means. In America, cider is fresh pressed apple juice. In England and Australia cider is fermented juice – what Americans call hard cider.

Where did oranges come from?
Oranges were first cultivated in India, China and Japan. After some eastern tinkering, the Chinese developed the mandarin and tangerine species. The lemon and the orange were brought West in the 15th century. After several centuries of western tinkering, the seedless navel orange appeared in the Mediterranean regions.

What is a grapefruit?
The grapefruit was developed in the 19th century as a cross between the orange and the pummelo, a large citrus fruit. The Ruby Red grapefruit was an unusual mutation found on the McAllen's Texas farm in 1929.

Do citrus fruits sweeten after picking?
Citrus contains almost no starch so it does not sweeten after it is picked. (In many fruits & seeds, starches eventually break down into sugars.) However, citrus fruits are commonly treated with the gas ethylene to improved color and waxed to reduce moisture loss.

What are the differences and varieties of the "stone" fruits?
The apricot, cherry, peach and plum are all "stone" fruits -- that is they have a singular seed (pit) within. The peach is classified in the two varieties: freestone and clingstone. As the names suggest, the difference is how easily the fruit separates from the stone. The nectarine is a fuzzy-less form of the peach but it is interesting to note that peaches and nectarines can spontaneously develop into one another in the seed or bud form.

Why are some peaches "mealy" tasting?
Ever have one of the really mealy peaches from the supermarket? They are mealy because the fruit was picked too early and was put into cold storage for several weeks (i.e. shipment). This process destroys the enzyme that would have otherwise converted the peaches' protopectin into pectin.

When is a fruit not a fruit?
Blackberries, raspberries and strawberries are called "false fruits" because the fruit forms at the base of the flower instead of the ovary. What appears to be seeds along the side of the fruit is actually another small fruit encapsulating an even smaller seed. (By definition, a fruit is formed of the plant's ovary and contains the seeds within.)

How do I choose a ripe melon?
Like the citrus, melons do not sweeten after picking so it is best to leave them on the vine as long as possible. When I buy a melon (particularly a watermelon) I thump it with my thumb and listen for a low, dead THUMP. The lower the "pitch" the better. I have never picked a bad melon when I do this (at the price of strange looks from other shoppers).

Where did cranberries originate?
Cranberries, one of the few fruits native to America, was cultivated beginning in 1840 in Massachusetts. Today about 50% of the USA crop is grown in the Bay State (Massachusetts).

Why is it traditional to bring a pineapple to a housewarming?
Pineapples are native to South America and were brought to Europe about 1535. One story tells of an explorer, upon returning to Europe, who brought a Pineapple to the Queen. Eventually, in memory of this event, it became the custom to bring a Pineapple as a housewarming gift. The image of the

pineapple arriving was meant to express the sense of welcome, good cheer, human warmth and family affection. In the 18th century the Pineapple was brought to Hawaii and today is the major fruit crop of Hawaii.

How do I choose a ripe pineapple?
The Pineapple is very picky about when it ripens, requiring specific temperatures and conditions. Sometime it will not ripen significantly, then quickly become over ripe. At the grocery store, select the pineapple that has the least amount of green on the skin and that makes a solid sound when thumped.

May I use fresh pineapple in gelatin?
No. The enzyme papain in fresh pineapple breaks down the gelatin into a liquid goop. Papain is also used in meat tenderizers because it breaks down (tenderizes) meat. However, the heat used in the pineapple canning process neutralizes the papain, thus, canned pineapple may be used in gelatin. (note: Kiwi fruit contains the enzyme actinidin which similarly affects gelatin.)

Vegetables

Where does the word "Vegetable" come from?
"Vegetable" comes from the Latin verb "vegere" meaning to enliven or animate.

Were Carrots always orange?
No. Carrots, native to Afghanistan, were purple, red and even black. In the 16th century, a yellow strain became popular, perhaps, because it would not color soups. A century later, an orange strain of carrot was developed in Holland. Colonists to the new world brought these seeds with them where some escaped cultivation and became the wildflower Queen Anne's Lace.

What makes radishes taste hot?
The skin of the radish has an enzyme that can form a mustard oil. Peeling the skin will reduce the hot taste.

Where did the potato come from?
The potato, a member or the nightshade family and thus related to the tomato and tobacco, originated in South and Central America. 4,000 years ago it was the staple food for the Incas because the hardy plant could grow at altitudes where corn could not.

Spanish Explorers brought the Sweet Potato, named batata by the Caribbean Indians, to Europe in 1570. Because the potato was hardy, easy to grow and yielded more energy per acre than wheat or barley, it became a staple food in Ireland.

Is the sweet potato and the yam the same type of potato?
No -- what is called a yam in the United States is actually a sweet potato. Sweet potatoes have smooth skin, orange or yellow flesh and a sweet taste. Yams (derived from the African word *nyami*) have rough and scaly skin, white flesh and taste starchy.

Why was the potato deemed poisonous?
The suspicion was not unfounded. The potato, a member of the poisonous nightshade family, does have poisonous leaves and sprouts. However, the French incorrectly believed the potato caused leprosy. Eventually King Louis XVI, convinced by a pharmacist of the potato's innocence, allowed the potato to be served in his court. The tuber quickly became all the rage throughout France. (Just try to imagine the world without French Fries!)

Can potatoes be poisonous?
The leaves and stems of potatoes contain the toxic alkaloid solanine. Green potatoes and sprouts also contain solanine. It's best to not use such potatoes, but if you must, deeply peel the skin. Since potatoes create solanine when exposed to light or at refrigerator temperatures, store them where it is dark and cool (but not too cool). If the potato sprouts during storage, dig the sprouts out when peeling the skin.

What potatoes are best for various dishes?
There are two basic types of potatoes: waxy and mealy. Mealy types, which crumble when cooked(i.e. Idaho, Russet), are better for mashed or baked potatoes. Waxy types (i.e. Maine,

general purpose) are best for scalloped potatoes or similar foods where the intent is to have the potato stay together.

Are Brussel Sprouts related to cabbage?
Brussel Sprouts are actually the buds that grow off the sides of the cabbage stem. The cabbage is the main bud at the top of the stem.

Are Rhubarb leaves poisonous?
Yes. The leaves have significant levels of Oxalic Acid. Oxalic Acid is present in common foods (potatoes, peas) and is also the product of metabolized Vitamin C. However, Rhubarb leaves have relatively high amounts. While only a small amount can cause illness, it would take about 11 pounds of ingested leaves to have a 50% chance of killing a 145 pound person. The stalks, often used in jams and pies, do contain Oxalic Acid but only in very small, safe, amounts.

How did Rhubarb get its name?
The name is a combination of the Greek "Rha" (as in the river) and the Latin "barbarum" meaning barbarians. It was these inhabitants of the Rha river region that used the plant. (Today the Rha is known as the Volga river.)

How did Rhubarb get to America?
Legend has it that Ben Franklin brought Rhubarb seeds from Europe to America in 1772.

Why does an Artichoke heart taste sweet?
The Artichoke, a member of the Daisy family, was popular in Rome and brought to America by Italian settlers. The name was derived from the Arabic name "al'qarshuf". The artichoke heart is actually a flower base. Were it allowed to bloom, it would be a deep violet flower. It was learned in 1954 that artichoke hearts contain *cynarin* (an organic acid) which stimulates the

sweet taste buds causing anything eaten shortly afterward to taste sweet. Try drinking some water after eating an artichoke heart. Does it taste sweet? For most people, it will.

Where did the Pumpkin get it's name from?
The pumpkin, originally from Central America, was named "pumpion" by the English. The name's foundation is from the Greek word *pepón*, meaning "large melon".

How can I store a pumpkin for a long time?
First wash the pumpkin with a solution of 1 tablespoon of chlorine bleach and 1 gallon of water to clear away and inoculate against mold and rot. Store the pumpkin in a cool (45°F to 60°F) dry place for up to 1 month or in the refrigerator for up to 3 months.

Where did the Eggplant come from?
The eggplant, a member of the Nightshade family, was native to India and brought to Spain and Africa by Arab traders. It was so named because of its egg shape and white color. (The more common purple eggplant was discovered later.)

How does one choose a good eggplant?
Look for a smooth skin and no brown or soft spots. Store in a cool place and use within 2 days.

Why does the eggplant absorb so much oil when cooked?
The soft tissue pockets of the eggplant soaks up oil as it is cooked much as a sponge soaks up water. However, once sufficiently heated, the tissue breaks down releasing the oil.

When do you pick a Green Pepper?
Before it turns color! Green peppers are unripe Sweet or Bell peppers. Once ripe they can be yellow, red, brown or purple.

What makes red chili peppers spicy?
The alkaloid capsaicin is responsible for making your eyes water and nose run. Capsaicin is used in pepper sprays (for self-defense) and can be found in various medications for arthritis and anti-inflammatories. It is also anti-bacterial and high in vitamin C.

What is the hottest pepper?
Hot peppers are rated on the Scoville scale developed by Wilbur Scoville when researching capsaicin for use in a muscle cream. The test includes mixing some amount of the pepper in a sugar and water concoction in decreasing amounts until it can no longer be tasted by a panel of taste testers. The higher the rating, the hotter the pepper! Sometime it is abbreviated SHU for Scoville Heat Units. There are always new hybrids of peppers but of the commonly available peppers, the Habanero brags the highest SHU.

Why do I feel good after eating really spicy peppers?
The capsaicin in hot peppers fools your brain into thinking you are in pain. The brain's natural response to pain is to release Endorphins – a natural analgesic which dulls pain and gives a mild feeling of euphoria.

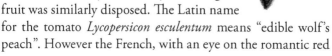

Were Tomatoes thought to be poisonous?
Native to the Andes Mountains, the tomato was first domesticated in Mexico then moved to Europe. The tomato's poisonous foliage and fellow poisonous Nightshade family members certainly had many believing its fruit was similarly disposed. The Latin name for the tomato *Lycopersicon esculentum* means "edible wolf's peach". However the French, with an eye on the romantic red

color, named it *pommes d'armour* meaning literally "apples of love".

Avocados

The Avocado, known as the "poor man's butter", is almost 20% monounsaturated fat. The name comes from the Latin American Nahuatl word *ahuacatl* which means "testicle". The Avacado is unique among fruits in that its sugar decreases during the ripening process and it cannot ripen without oxygen.

How do you select a good Avocado?

Look for an Avocado with a uniform texture and feels heavy for its size. If it has a bruise, soft spot or when shaken the pit comes loose, look further.

How do you ripen an Avocado?

Put it in a paper bag and let sit at room temperature for 2-5 days. Adding a banana or apple will accelerate the ripening process. Do not put it in the refrigerator during ripening.

Why does Gumbo and other Southern US recipes call for Okra?

The Okra plant, brought to the US from Africa during the slave trade, contains long carbohydrate molecules. These mucilaginous molecules are useful for thickening soups (eg. gumbo) and sauces.

How are black olives and green olives related?

A green olive (sometimes called the Spanish olive) is an unripe black olive.

What's the difference between grades of olive oil?

To extract olive oil, the olives are pressed. The first pressing extracts the best tasting oil with the lowest amount of oleic acid. This is called "extra virgin" (up to 1% oleic acid) or "virgin" (up to 4% oleic acid) olive oil. Subsequent pressings will generally require further refining to remove harsh flavors and are often labeled as "pure".

Why are Greek olives so bitter?
Any green (unripe) raw olive is bitter due the presence of oleropein. This substance is removed by soaking in lye then washed. The Greek olives are not processed in a lye bath and hence they taste quite bitter.

How else are olives processed?
Ripe olives and green olives run through a lye-bath are then cured either in oil, water, brine (salt water) or by drying. Generally, the longer the olive is cured, the less bitter and more intricate the flavor.

Why are so many chemicals (i.e. drugs, poisons) found in plants?
Since plants can't run away from their hungry predators, nearly all of them have developed chemical compounds meant to discourage their consumption. We humans have learned to manipulate the plants and reduce their chemical side effects. Or, in a few other cases, plants are developed to maximize their side effects giving us drugs which range from caffeine to lysergic acid diethylamide (LSD).

How do the chemical compounds in plants stop animals from consuming the plants?
Alkaloids are alkaline-containing complexes that disrupt animal metabolism. In small quantities, like caffeine and nicotine, the side effect is stimulation. But in high levels, like in green potatoes and potato sprouts, the alkaloids can be

deadly. (A little green in a potato is OK, but avoid the green sprouts. If you take a bite with a high level of alkaloids, you will notice a burning sensation on your tongue.)

Fruits are good to eat but how about the seeds?
Since plants can't move, one way to spread their seeds around is to tempt animals to eat the fruit containing seeds. The animals carry away the seeds in their bellies and later excrete the seeds in their metabolic waste. The trick is for the seeds to not be crushed during consumption and survive digestion. Some plants protect their seeds with poison so that animals learn not to crush them. One example of these poisons are Cyanogens which are cyanide complexes found in a number of fruit seeds; apple, cherry, pear, peach, apricot, and plum. Eating a few seeds containing these respiratory inhibitors may not hurt you. Avoid eating them none-the-less! There are records of people having died from eating a few dozen roasted apple seeds.

Do you have a good excuse to avoid eating Lima Beams?
Cyanogens are also found in other plants such as lima & kidney beans (you always wanted a reason to hate them anyway), yams, sweet potatoes and bamboo shoots. Today, these plants are bred to minimize the cyanide content and boiling them helps in getting rid of the remaining amounts. The boiling works best if you leave the cover off so the escaping hydrogen cyanide gas (the "stink" you smell when beans are cooking) leaves as soon as it is formed.

Is it true that nutmeg is a drug?
Myristicin (a hallucinogen) found in nutmeg is said to have been the drug of choice for Malcom X and Charlie Parker. A little nutmeg grated onto your eggnog or fettuccini alfredo won't hurt you though. Similarly, toxic oils, such as thujone and myristicin, are found in nutmeg, mace, black pepper, carrot, parsley, and celery seeds. Not to fret – under normal use, these oils do not present any danger.

Banana peels are a drug too?
Banana peels contain the neuro-drugs serotonin, dopamine and norepinephrine. This encouraged a few oddballs in the 1960s to try smoking the peels. Good thing this didn't catch on.

What foods should I avoid if I have a thyroid gland problem?
Goitrins interfere with intake of iodine, necessary for the thyroid gland. So if you have a thyroid condition, stay away from cabbage and cauliflower.

Should I eat raw beans?
Raw beans contain protease inhibitors and lectins that interfere with digestion by preventing nutrient absorbtion and overstimulation of the pancreas. Eating beans raw is not a good idea. Fortunately, boiling rids the beans of these compounds.

Mushrooms

What are Mushrooms?
Mushrooms are fungi and are related to molds and yeast. They cannot make sugar from light (photosynthesis) as most other plants, instead they feed off of decaying organisms. Their structure is comprised of the compound *chitin (pronc. kite-in)*, which also comprises the outer skeleton of insects and crustaceans.

What are Truffles?
Truffles are fungi that grow in symbiosis with certain tree roots (i.e. oaks, hazelnut). Their high content of glutamic acid (similar to MSG (monosodium glutamate)) intensifies any dish to which it is added.

Why are pigs utilized to find truffles?
The pigs can smell the musky chemical truffles produce because the chemical, also found in a pig's saliva, is a boar's pheromone.

Do chocolate truffles contain real truffles?
No. The chocolate treats known as truffles are named such because with their size and round, rough surface they look like the mushroom truffles.

How should one store mushrooms?
Mushrooms lose much of their sugar and starch to chitin four

days after harvest. Keeping the mushrooms in refrigeration and in airtight wrapping will slow down, but not stop, this conversion. Thus, it is best to use them as soon as possible.

How can you identify poisonous mushrooms?
Only an expert can tell for certain, but characteristics of poisonous mushrooms includes having warts or scales on the cap, gills which are white or light colored, a ring on the upper or lower stem and a stem base shaped like a bulb. Mushroom poisoning can appear right away or hours or even days later. IF MUSHROOMS OF UNKNOWN TYPE ARE CONSUMED, CONTACT A DOCTOR OR POISON CONTROL CENTER IMMEDIATELY. IF POSSIBLE, PUT ON GLOVES AND DIG UP SOME OF THE MUSHROOM TO SHOW TO MEDICAL PERSONNEL.

Starch

What is starch and what does it do for foods?
Starch (a germanic word for "stiff") is a long chain of sugar molecules that is found in flour, corn, potatoes and other vegetables and cereals. It is used in gravies and sauces because at about 145 Deg F it begins to gelatinize, thickening the sauce or gravy. Often the starch is browned in a fat (such as butter, oil, bacon drippings) before combining with liquid. This is to reduce the "dry" taste of the starch and adds a nutty flavor instead. (The rue [roux] in gumbo is a good example of this.)

Starch Tip #1: If you are making a sauce with starch and it is not thick enough, do NOT add more starch (flour/cornstarch) directly to the mixture. This will lead to lumps. Instead, mix a tablespoon or so of the starch to a few tablespoons of COLD water. Then whisk the heated sauce while slowly adding the mixture. Also, the sauce will thicken slightly as it cools.

Starch Tip #2: A common mistake is to put food with high starch levels in the refrigerator for long periods of time. It turns out that starch expels water at about 34 Deg F -- which is just about the temperature of your refrigerator! What this means is that breads will dry out and gravies will become a lump swimming in a pool of water. To avoid this, it is a much better idea to store breads, gravies and other high starch cooked or baked foods in the freezer.

Bread

What makes bread rise?

Bread is leavened (made to rise) by trapping gas (carbon dioxide) inside pockets of dough. Today we use cultured yeast to eat flour and make the gas, but long ago yeast was captured by mixing flour and water and waiting for the yeast to move in, munch  away and multiply. Once a culture is started, it is kept going by simply replacing the flour/water mixture used in bread.

What is yeast?

Yeast is a single-celled fungus plant. It feeds on sugar and starch and creates carbon dioxide and alcohol (eats without sunlight as would be true of any fungus). One ounce of fresh yeast contains over a quarter billion cells. If the yeast were placed under ideal conditions for 5 days, that one ounce of yeast would grow into 21 tons of yeast!

Yeast tip: You have to have good yeast! Bakers "proof" the yeast by mixing it with water, a little flour and waiting about 5 minutes to see if the yeast begins to make bubbles. If few or no bubbles, it is bad yeast. To ensure good yeast, buy a large cake of yeast and store it in a sealed container in the freezer. It can keep up to a year this way and it will always be good so no "proof"ing is required.

Bread Tip #1: Where possible, mix all the ingredients at or slightly above room temperature. If possible, use water with the chlorine filtered out and at about 100° F. (Chlorine retards the yeast growth.)

Bread tip #2: Spices (eg. cinnamon, nutmeg, cardamom) and salt tends to inhibit yeast growth, so do not expect those breads to rise as well. Sugar will help yeast rise, but too much sugar will make the yeast sluggish and the bread will not rise. If your diet calls for less salt, cut the recipe's suggested salt in half and you will see the bread rise much higher.

How do I know if the dough has the right mixture of flour and water?
If the dough is hard and smooth, add a tablespoon or two of water, mix it in and recheck. If the dough is mushy and sticks to your fingers, add several tablespoons of flour. Recheck the dough during kneading and add flour or water as needed. The dough is just right when the feel of the dough is soft, tacky and does not come off on your fingers.

Why does bread need to be kneaded?
Bread rises because the pressure of the carbon dioxide (CO_2) gas (created by the yeast consuming the flour and sugar) pushes against the "woven" gluten/starch in the bread. The "weave" is a result of the bread dough having been kneaded. So here's the catch: if the dough is kneaded too little, the "weave" will not be tight, the gas will escape and you have flat bread. If the dough is kneaded too much, the "weave" is too strong and the gas pressure is insufficient to cause the bread to rise.

When and where were the beginnings of sourdough bread?
Can you imagine passing by some lady in ancient Egypt (circa 4000 B.C.) sniffing some spoiled flour/water mixture and declaring, "Great Ibis! This stuff stinks! I think I'll bake it over the coals and see what it tastes like..." No one is really certain

how and when leavened bread got its start but this is probably not far from sourdough bread's origins. Sourdough was the first type of leavened bread because yeast was not understood and thus not cultivated as it was much later.

Why does sourdough taste sour and regular yeast bread does not? Like bakers yeast, it converts the flour and water mixture into many byproducts including gasses (i.e. carbon dioxide) but sourdough yeast can live in more acidic environments. Sourdough takes more time to work and will create "hooch" -- an alcoholic liquid that rises to the top of the sourdough crock. However, it is the lactic acid which gives the sourdough its unique flavor and is dependent on the type of yeast and hence, the location. For example, a very sharp yeast, Lactobacillus sanfrancisco, is found only in the San Francisco area and is responsible for the famous San Francisco sourdough breads.

Sourdough bread tip: Sometimes recipe books recommend spraying bread dough with water before/during baking to give it a thick chewy crust. This author's experience is that this does not work. Instead, try putting a large pan of water (about 1" inch water) in the oven as it warms up. The steam from the pan in the oven will thicken the crust during baking. Alternatively, baking stones work well even without the pan of water. You can use inexpensive untreated, unglazed ceramic tiles (found at some hardware stores) for the baking stone. I find 4 tiles per rack works well. When arranged in a square, the 4 tiles have a width of 14". Garner a 14" pizza peel and some parchment paper and you are all set to make brick oven sourdough bread and pizza.

Meet Meat

In 900 AD the term "meat" meant any solid food. Still today, for example, we call the edible part of a nut the "meat". By about 1300 AD, meat designated the flesh of animals. It is a good thing humans are not carnivores because there has not been enough land and natural resources for a long time to feed us exclusively on meat. On the other hand, meat provides several necessary amino acids (protein building blocks), which the herbivores (a.k.a. vegetarians) among us struggle to include in their diets.

How much protein is in meat?
Meat contains approximately 75% liquid, 18% protein and 3% fat. Of common meats, the leanest, most protein rich meat is chicken followed by fish then turkey, beef, lamb and pork. (Of course the type of cut makes a difference.)

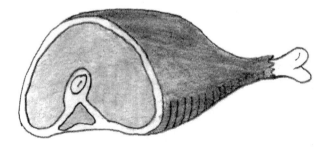

How should one cut meat to maximize tenderness?
Meat is made up of long, thin muscle fibers bound together by connective tissue. The longitude structure of muscle bundles

is what we call the grain. When carving meat, especially less tender cuts, cut across the grain makes chewing easier.

Does the method of slaughter affect the taste of the meat?
How an animal is slaughtered does make a difference in the taste of the meat. If the animal is well treated and the slaughter is quick and painless as possible, the meat will contain fewer chemical byproducts from stress, thus improving flavor, texture and storage. The Jewish Kosher process, for example, regulates animal slaughter in this way. Certainly they realize that these more humane methods have a culinary benefit also.

Why do they hang beef sides after slaughter?
The post-mortem chemical process causes the meat to contract and toughen. The solution is to hang beef on a rack after slaughter. Hanging the beef counteracts the rigor mortis by keeping the meat stretched out and hence more tender. Not all meats benefit from extended hanging, but aging beef by hanging the beef sides for two to four weeks at near freezing temperatures makes for tender and more flavorful meat.

Is the red "juice" I see on my beef plate blood?
No. There is very little blood left in the meat by the time it reaches the dinner table. The red myoglobin, which held the oxygen for the muscle, taints the beef liquid red.

Why is pork meat white, but ham is pink?
Ham is certainly pork, and if it isn't cured, it would be white like all other pork. The difference is that ham is treated ("cured") with nitrites. The nitrites react with the meat's myoglobin causing a color change.

Are nitrites good or bad?
Nitrites can be carcinogenic (i.e. cancer causing agents) and even toxic in high levels. However, they also prevent botulism,

and used carefully in the prescribed manner, are very safe. Most people consider the benefits to outweigh the risks.

In general, can you tell the meat's tenderness by its location in the animal?
Cuts of meat vary in tenderness. As a rule-of-thumb, the farther the cut from the hoof or horns, the more tender the meat. Tender cuts are best cooked broiling (high heat such as coals), frying or roasting. Less tender cuts (such as a pot roast) requires moist cooking in a stew pot or crock pot. The moisture helps break down the less tender muscle bundles for easier chewing.

How do I choose tender chicken?
Age is the key. Young chicken (roasters, hens) go in the oven. Older chickens (fowl, stew) go in the pot of water. If roasting a chicken, set the oven to 350 deg F but if you stuff it, set the oven to 325 deg F. The lower temperature makes sure the inside stuffing and outer meat reaches a safe temperature together. In general, the quicker the meat is cooked the less moisture it will lose so the more juicy and tender the meat will be. If you want the best tasting bird, don't stuff it!

What is a Capon?
There is a little known chicken roaster called a "capon" which is a young castrated male. Allegedly the Capon puts more energy into growth than chasing the ladies (hens) around the chicken run. Reportedly this chicken yields very tender meat. This author's singular attempt to cook a Capon did not agree with the conventional wisdom.

Why is some meat light and some dark?
Dark meat comes from the part of the animal, which must sustain small, long term motion (slow cells) and light (white) meat is found in the muscles which must provide short bursts

of power (fast cells). The slow cells burn fat and require oxygen (aerobic respiration). The fast cells burn glycogen and can do so, if need be, without oxygen (anaerobic respiration). So for example, this would explain why chicken legs (for walking) are dark meat and the breast is white (for flapping wings). Fish meat follows the same pattern where the meat near the skin, for long-term slow movement, is dark, but the inner meat is white and is used to provide quick speed.

Should I let the meat sit out before roasting?
If the meat you are going to roast is refrigerated, take it out about an hour before placing it in the oven to come up to room temperature. This will result in less cooking time and a more uniform texture. Do not leave it out for more than 2 hours or the bacteria will flourish!

Where do you put a meat thermometer?
Bones do not conduct heat as well as meat, so placing the thermometer near a bone will give a false indication. Place the thermometer in the center of the meat keeping it away from the bones. The "pop-up" timers, often included with chicken or turkey, put safety ahead of taste. They will pop typically when the breast meat reaches 180 to 190 Deg F. The meat is thoroughly cooked, to be sure, but the meat is rather dry. Use a meat thermometer and remove the bird when the temperature reaches 165 Deg F. After removal from the oven, the internal temperature will continue to rise another 10 deg F. (See carving tips below)

Should I let the roasted meat sit before carving?
When you take meat out of the oven, let it sit 10 to 20 minutes before carving. During cooking, the muscle fibers are stretched tight squeezing out the moisture into the space surrounding the fibers. If you cut the meat when hot, the moisture will ooze and steam away and you are left with dry meat. Let the meat

rest and cool. Doing so will allow the meat to re-absorb much of the moisture and hold it better during carving. Also, use a sharp knife (not serrated!). Besides, resting the roast gives you time to pop in those dinner rolls and make gravy too!

How long should meat stay out at room temperature after cooking?
Unpreserved meat requires food safety consideration. The rule of thumb is no more than 2 hours between 40° F and 140° F: Any longer and the bacteria count increases sharply. So refrigerate meat after two hours, if not sooner. Preserved meats such as ham and salami can stay out of refrigeration longer.

How was meat preserved before refrigeration?
It is hard for us today to imagine the effort it took to preserve meat for days, weeks or months. The goal of preservation is to make the meat uninhabitable to bacteria but palatable to people. In the days before refrigeration, essentially four methods were used to preserve meat: 1) Salting – Salt was rubbed into the meat repeatedly 2) Drying – hanging the meats in very dry, moving air. 3) Spicing – spices were rubbed into the meat repeatedly. 4) Smoking – meats were smoked over low heat. The other advantage to meat preservation was the flavor added by the process.

What is lard?
Lard is clarified pork fat. Where the fat comes from on the pig determines the quality of the lard. The highest quality of lard comes from the fat surrounding the internal organs called "leaf lard". Lard is well suited for pastries yielding flaky crusts. When using lard in place of butter, reduce the amount by about 25%. One of the byproducts of making lard are those tasty little brown crispies known as cracklings.

What is suet?

Suet is the fat from livestock (i.e. cow, sheep) found around the kidney and loin areas. Popular recipes around England call for suet to richen puddings, pastries, and mincemeats. Suet can also be used to make tallow candles and soaps.

Why are meats "brined"?

The brining process involves soaking meats in a mixture of water, salt, sugar, acid (eg. vinegar) and optionally, spices. The salt and sugar helps the meat draw in more water and hold it better. The acidic component helps to tenderize the meat. Spices add flavor. The end result is more flavorful and tender meat. Brining works best with meats that typically cook up dry (e.g. turkey, pork).

Where does the word Sausage come from?

The word sausage comes from the Latin word "*salsus*" meaning salted meat. Essentially, all sausage is chopped or ground meat, most is stuffed into a casing of some sort. Typically, sausage makers add spices and herbs to add flavor and dry or smoke to preserve the sausage.

Where did Sausage making originate?

Livestock owners in the Near East were the first to preserve meat by salting meat scraps and stuffing it in casing (made from animal intestines) and other animal organs. The pig, domesticated about 5000BC in Egypt and China, became the source of most sausages. Raising pigs (and sausage making) spread from the Near East to Europe and Asia.

Basic tips for sausage making:
Use fresh meats. Adding fat or using fatty cuts of meat improves juiciness and flavor. Use fresh spices. Keep the meat and equipment clean and store finished sausage properly. The colder the meat the better the sausage grinds and extrudes. Add 1 lb of liquid (about 16oz) for every 10 lb of sausage meat to improve moistness and extrude better. The liquid can be water, or complimentary flavors of beer, wine, or fruit juice.

What are the various types of sausage?
Some are fresh (Polish sausage, Italian sausage, frankfurters), some are smoked (andouille, kielbasa) some are cooked (bologna, liverwurst) and some are not cooked but cured (salami, pepperoni).

Is cured meat raw?
Some of our most popular sausages (eg. salami, pepperoni) contain meat that is not cooked. The raw meats are cured (preserved) using a combination of sodium nitrite and sodium nitrate. High levels of these preservatives can be dangerous, even fatal, but without them, you can get botulism from the bacteria *Clostridium botulinum*. Thus, the amounts used are measured with great precision. If you make you own cured meats, use a cure premixed by professionals and follow the instructions precisely. If you think eating raw meat is rather disgusting, don't speak with your mouth full of prosciutto (also uncooked, cured meat).

What is a summer sausage?
Summer Sausage is a "dry sausage". This type of sausage is fermented by the lactic acid within which gives the summer sausage its tangy flavor.

Why does fish flesh cook so much faster than animal flesh?
Fish do not need a lot of connective tissue or fat because they

1) do not have to fight gravity and 2) are cold blooded. Thus, with less connective tissue and little fat, fish flesh cooks quicker and can be more easily overcooked.

Why do lobster and crab shell change color when cooked?
The chemical that yields the characteristic red color of cooked crustaceans is always present even before cooking. However, before cooking the chemical astaxanthin is combined in a compound that makes it look greenish. The high heat separates the astaxanthin from the compound and the red hue appears. Someone should please inform Hollywood and the seafood industry of this fact because never, to the knowledge of this author, has an animated crab or lobster ever seen as anything but red. Tell them, "If it's red, it must be dead!"

Herbs & Spices

The theory is that spices (specifically the oils and chemicals which give spices their flavors) were a plant's evolutionary effort to resist consumption by animals and bacteria. From the human perspective spices added wonderful flavors to food, were great for preserving food and also found use as early forms of medicine. Here are some of the interesting facts about today's common spices:

Basil: From the Latin word basiliscus referring to the basilisk, a fire breathing dragon. This perhaps stems from the belief that this spice is a charm used against the beast. Used to flavor the liquor Chartreuse

Marjoram: The sweet version has a more delicate flavor while the wild, more bitter, version is sold as oregano.

Oregano: From the Greek for "mountain joy". Not seen in America until the 1950's when the GI's returned from Italy and insisted on sprinkling some on their pizza.

Peppermint: Contains the remarkable chemical, menthol. Menthol, when placed on the skin, raises the threshold temperature at which the cold receptors begin to discharge. For example, menthol makes our warm mouth feel cold because the "cold" sensors in the mouth now think that body temperature is cold and they send less "it's hot here" signals to the brain. In large doses, Menthol has anesthetic properties.

Rosemary: From the Latin meaning "sea dew", this evergreen shrub was used by the Romans primarily in medicine but goes well with meat (especially good with lamb).

Sage: Another medicinal herb used by the Greeks & Romans and later by the English as steeped in hot water before they were introduced to tea.

Thyme: From the Greek "to burn sacrifice" and used since classical times as a fumigant and antiseptic. It is active against salmonella and staphylococcus bacteria and is used to flavor the liqueur Benedictine.

Anise: If you have ever quaffed ouzo, you have had anise. The Greeks, Romans and Hebrews used Anise as a condiment. One compound found in licorice root is glycyrrhizin, which is 50 times sweeter than sugar. Anise is the key flavor in the Italian pizzelle and licorice candy.

Caraway: The seeds of which were found in dwellings dated 8,000 years old in central Europe. Still popular in Europe it is used to flavor breads, cheese, meat, vegetables and liqueurs.

Coriander: Sanskrit and papyri records indicate that this spice has been around for 5,000 years. 17th century Paris found it all the rage in a concoction, which doubled as a cologne and a liqueur. (What's the French word for "Sip-n-Splash"?)

Cumin: Mentioned in the Bible, Cumin finds it's home in Indian Curry, European breads and its largest producer is Iran.

Fennel: Cultivated by the Egyptians, its name refers to a type of fragrant hay. Used in sweets, liquors and breads. If you sprinkle a little fennel, salt and pepper over ground pork you have a basic sweet Italian sausage.

Parsley: Greeks used this spice for medicine and crowns for victorious athletes. Our word comes from the Greek petroselinum "rock-celery" which refers to its natural rocky habitat.

What is the difference between black, white and green pepper?
All these peppers come from the same tropical berries but are processed differently. Native to India, young pepper berries are picked from the vine when they are green then dried under the sun (green pepper). Some green berries are exposed to a black fungus (*glomerella cingulata*), which sets in and causes the berries to turn black, making black pepper. If the mature red berries are picked then the berries are soaked in water and the skins and pulp are rubbed off until the white seeds remain (white pepper). This yields milder (white) pepper and is most useful as a seasoning for white sauces.

What gives black and white pepper its kick?
The alkaloid piperine.

Coffee

How did coffee get its start?

Coffee (a.k.a. Kahwah, Kahue, Kaffe, Café), according to legend, was discovered by the Arabian Khalifah Al-Kulab in 291 when he noticed that goats who ate certain berries did not want to bed down at night. Boiling the berry's beans in water, he learned, stimulated him. As the Arabs began to export their new-found brew they decided to bake the seeds so that no one else could grow the bush. As luck would have it, roasting the beans added more flavor to the brew.

How do you know that this is the genesis of coffee?

I don't. It's a legend. There are a number of other legends, which speak of Arabians of other names at other times. Some other legends attribute the discovery to a monk who was trying to come up with a way to keep other monks from falling asleep during evening prayers when he took notice of the frisky, berry eating goats. Still others say it was the Arabian who gave it to the monk.

How do I brew the perfect cup of coffee?

Start with whole coffee beans you have been storing in the freezer. Use 2 tablespoons of coffee beans ground fine for each 6 oz cup of coffee. Grind them fine but not to a powder. Expose the grinds to 200ºF (93ºC) water for two minutes then filter out the liquid. If you want weaker coffee than this, rather than use less coffee or shorter brew times, just add some hot water to this recipe.

Is it better to use drip or percolation coffee brewing?
It is generally considered that the drip method brews the better pot perhaps because the drip method better approximates the process outlined above. Percolation exposes the grinds to hot water and steam for 10-15 minutes and this brings out a more bitter flavor.

How long can coffee stay in the pot and still taste fresh?
About 20 minutes. After that, the coffee begins to taste noticeably more bitter.

Are all coffee beans the same?
There are about a dozen types of coffee beans. The most common bean is *Coffea Arabica* which accounts for about 75% of all coffees and contains the lowest levels of caffeine. The second most popular bean is *Coffea canephora* which is also known as Robusta coffee. Robusta has twice the caffeine of arabica and a bitter taste, but is less expensive to produce, so it is considered a lower grade of coffee.

How is caffeine removed from coffee?
In 1903 a German chemist (Ludwig Roselius) learned that the solvent methylene chloride removes caffeine from coffee without affecting other components of coffee. This decaffeinated coffee was eventually marketed as Sanka, which was a contraction of *sans caffeine.* Although the levels of methylene chloride in decaf coffee are well within FDA guidelines, there are other methods today which avoid using this known carcinogen. Today's methods also use water, ethyl acetate (found naturally in fruits) and carbon dioxide processes to remove caffeine from the bean.

What is Kopi coffee?
Kopi Luwak coffee is made from beans that have undergone
a most interesting alteration. The Asia Palm Civet is a weasel
like animal that has a fond taste for the cherries of the coffee
tree. The seeds (beans) of the fruit pass through the Civet
and are excreted as part of their metabolic waste. This waste
is collected, washed, lightly roasted and ground into coffee.
Some believe the digestive enzymes of the Civet affect the
beans flavor during their intestinal travel. Others say it is the
Civet's selection in picking the choicest berries. In the end, this
coffee is the most expensive coffee in the world, selling for up
to $600 USD per pound.

How did Tea get its start?
Chinese legend claims that Emperor Shen Nung had observed
that people who boiled their drinking water were generally
healthier. One day, in 2737 BC, some leaves fell into his pot
of boiling water. Noticing the wonderful aroma the leaves
brought to the pot, he decided to take a sip of the brew. The
rest, as they say, is history.

Where did Iced Tea get its start?
In 1904 the young Englishman, Richard Blechynden, was
having a hard time selling his hot tea. No wonder! He was at
an Exposition during a hot St. Louis summer! Desperate after
days of no sales, he decided to pour the tea over ice and put
chunks of ice in the glasses. The cooler, refreshing drink was
immediately popular and iced tea found its way into America's
summer fare.

Do different teas come from different leaves?
All tea is from the same plant, the only differences are where
it is grown and how it is processed. Once the leaves are picked
they are processed into the three basic tea groups: Green, Black
and Oolong. Green tea is just-picked leaves that are steamed to

prevent oxidation. Black tea starts with leaves which are dried and then crushed to allow the enzymes and the leaf cells to mix with oxygen producing various colored tannic complexes. This yields the unique taste and color of each tea. The Oolong tea processed similar to the Black tea but with less oxidation time.

Is the caffeine in tea and chocolate the same as in coffee?
Although closely related, there are slight chemical differences between the types of caffeine found in coffee [caffeine], tea [theophylline] and chocolate [theobromine]. Consequently, these different chemical structures result in varying effects on humans.

Does Green Tea have caffeine?
Yes, as does Oolong and Black teas.

How can I remove caffeine from tea?
An easy trick to remove most caffeine from tea is to drop the tea into just boiled water for about 30 seconds or run hot water (about 185°F (85°C)) through the tea for about 10-15 seconds before steeping. Caffeine needs a minimum water temperature of 175°F (79°C) to dissolve. Discard this water and replace it with more just boiled water. Soak the teabag for about 1 minute longer than usual to draw out an equal flavor. Caffeine is mostly on the outside of the leaves and most washes away before much of the flavor does.

What are the commercial processes used to remove caffeine from tea?
There are generally three methods: Methylene Chloride, Ethyl Acetate and Super Critical Carbon Dioxide. The first two are chemicals which remove caffeine (and some of the flavor). Only slight trace amounts (less than 10 parts per million) of the chemicals might remain at the end of the process and are not harmful at these levels (although Methylene chloride is carcinogenic at higher concentrations). The super critical

carbon dioxide method uses carbon dioxide gas under great pressure (under pressure, CO_2 is a liquid). The liquid CO_2 is washed over the tea leaves, removing the caffeine and leaving almost all the flavor.

Chocolate

Where did chocolate get its start?
The cocoa tree originated in South America and was migrated north into Mexico by the Aztecs/Incas/Mayas. The Cacao tree fruit grows off the trunk. The small melon fruit and the pulp inside contain 20 to 50 beans. (It takes about 400 beans to make a pound of chocolate.) The natives ground the roasted cocoa seeds (sometimes adding red pepper and vanilla) and mixed the grinds with hot water. It is reported that the Aztec emperor Montezuma drank 50 goblets of hot chocolate, flavored with chili peppers, every day.

What did Europe do when cocao beans arrived?
As this cocao bean mixture was introduced to Europe it became known as chocolate -- a word derived from the South American terms for "cocoa water" and "bitter water". Shying away from Montezuma's red pepper accent, the Europeans added other spices to their chocolate including sugar, cinnamon, anise, almonds, hazelnuts and cloves.

The novel beverage caught on and eventually the Europeans became addicted to the chocolate caffeine, theobromine – which derived from the greek words "theo" and "brosis" means "food of the gods". It became hard to not have that cup of chocolate in the morning. (Although the effect of theobromine on humans is much weaker than coffee's caffeine.) Here's a true story, which illustrates this addiction:

In Chiapa Real, Spain (now called San Cristobal de las Casas) the predominately female congregation at morning

Mass, needing their caffeine "fix", would actually have their maids bring them cups of chocolate during Mass. The Bishop, annoyed at this disturbance during the service, promised to excommunicate anyone who ate or drank during Mass. This created an uproar to the point that swords were drawn when priests tried to stop the maids from delivering the cups of chocolate. Soon afterward the Bishop died quite suddenly and his physician suspected poison. Local lore said it was a lethally prepared cup of chocolate. This gave rise to the Spanish proverb, "Beware the chocolate in Chiapa."

Why should pets not eat chocolate?
Never give a dog or cat chocolate, as it contains theobromine (a type of caffeine and central nervous system stimulant). As little as 2 ounces can be lethal to a small dog. (One ounce of chocolate contains about 20 mg of caffeine). Humans can breakdown theobromine quickly so we avoid the ill-effects suffered by pets who can't. In fact, the more typical human physiologic response to theobromine is to release serotonin which creates a feeling of pleasure.

What is the difference between Bittersweet and Semisweet chocolate?
Bittersweet chocolate is what is usually called for in baking. It contains more chocolate liquor (at least 35%) and less sugar than sweet chocolate.
Semisweet chocolate contains 15% - 35% chocolate liquor.

I don't have any semisweet or bittersweet chocolate on hand… can I use unsweetened chocolate and add sugar?
No. Unsweetened chocolate contains more fat and thus cooks differently than the sweetened chocolates.

Does milk chocolate really contain milk?
Yes. The added milk diminishes the bitterness of the chocolate liquor, much in the same way adding milk to tea or coffee make it less bitter.

What is Dutch chocolate?
Also known as "European-style" chocolate, Dutch chocolate is chocolate treated with an alkali. The process causes the chocolate to turn reddish brown and softens the bitter flavor. Devil's food cake is an example of this effect. Dutch chocolate is so named because it was invented by a Dutchman, Conrad van Houten.

What is White Chocolate?
It is cacao bean fat mixed with milk and sugar. It does not have the complex chocolate flavor because it lacks the bean's brown solids but it also has essentially none of the caffeine.

Alternate Chocolate tip:
If you are allergic to chocolate, do not like the caffeine, or your Bishop will not let you drink chocolate during Mass, you may wish to use the chocolate substitute: Carob. Carob has less bitter flavor than chocolate, less fat and calories and

no caffeine. Many health food stores carry carob powder and carob candy.

Can I use carob instead of chocolate in recipes?
You can substitute equal parts of carob for chocolate in recipes.

Where does carob come from?
Carob is the seed from an eastern Mediterranean evergreen tree. The carob tree is sometimes known as locust or St. John's bread, from the lore that the "locusts" which John the Baptist ate in the wilderness was actually carob pods.

Is there a relationship between Carob and the carats used to weigh diamond and gold?
The carob tree yields small pods that look much like pea pods containing beans. These carob beans of are very uniform in size and weight and became a tool for accurately measuring precious gems and metals. For example, a Roman coin that weighed the same as 24 carob beans was said to be 24 carat gold; a 12 carat coin was only 50% gold.

Onion & Garlic

Where did onions originate?
Onions have been cultivated since about 3,000 BC in the lands stretching from India to Israel. The word onion comes from the latin "unio" which means large pearl. Middle English changed this to "unyon".

Which American city was named after an onion?
The Algonquian Indian name for "onion place" is "Chicagoua" which became the name for the city of Chicago.

What in onions makes our eyes tear?
When you are chopping or slicing an onion, it releases the lachrymator (term for a chemical that produces tears) puruvate, into the air and mixes with your eye fluids forming sulfuric acid.

How can I lessen the onion tears?
Refrigerate the onion for an hour or so before cutting. The cold onion will release less puruvate into the air.

Why are sweet onions so sweet?
Sweet onions (eg. Vidalia, Texas 1015, Walla Walla) have a high sugar content. Due to this high sugar content, they spoil more rapidly than other onions so keep sweet onions in a dry, cool, and dark place with plenty of air circulation.

Why are onions more palatable when cooked?
The high heat not only rids the onion of its odor compounds but it converts some of its chemicals into a molecule that is as much as 70 times sweeter than table sugar.

What are the differences between yellow, white and red onions?
All-purpose yellow onions have a sharp taste and will not break apart in soups. White onions have a mild flavor and are used in salsa and sautés. Red onions, the sweetest of the three, lose their color when heated so they go best on salads and cold subs.

I've heard there are some fairly unusual laws concerning onions?
There are certainly strange onion laws out there. Some laws make little sense: It is illegal to eat onions with a spoon (Okanogan, WA), It is illegal to eat onion while drinking buttermilk on the Sabbath (Hackberry, AZ) and if a woman in Wolf Point, MT eats a raw onion on the Sabbath, her husband must follow her at 20 paces with a loaded musket. Other laws make more sense: It is illegal to enter a movie theater after eating an onion (Dyersburg, TN) and it is legal to throw onions at a persistent "obnoxious salesman" in Tamarack, Idaho.

Garlic
The slang names for garlic are almost as flavorful as the bulb itself; The Stinking Rose, Bronx vanilla, Halitosis and Italian perfume. In actuality, the name comes from the Old English *garleac* meaning "spear leek".

What makes garlic's unique smell?
When garlic is sliced, the chemical cysteine (which contains sulfur) mixes with an enzyme (allinaise) which together releases ammonia, pyruvic acid and daillyl disulfide (the primary odor).

I ate garlic soup last night and everyone is avoiding me today. Why?
The sulfur molecules from garlic are absorbed into the blood stream and escape, over time, through respiration and perspiration. Continued ingestion of garlic can cause a garlic body odor. It's best not to eat 40-clove garlic chicken before a long board meeting.

After peeling garlic, how do I get rid of the smell on my hands?
After washing your hands, rub them on something chrome (like a faucet).

It is a good idea to flavor oil by dropping garlic cloves into it?
Garlic is low in acid and may allow dangerous bacteria to grow if stored for a long time. If you must infuse garlic into oil or vinegar, best to store it in the refrigerator.

Is garlic good for your health?
The Telugu people from south-east India have the saying, "Garlic is as good as ten mothers." What they are trying to say is that garlic can help keep you healthy. In fact Garlic has been shown to be not only an anti-bacterial, but also helpful in lowering bad (LDL) cholesterol and thinning blood to reduce risks of stroke and heart attack.

What is a Shallot?
Named for the town (Askalon in South Palestine) where it was traded, it is a type of onion but has a milder flavor. Some describe the flavor as a cross between onion and garlic. It's most often used when a gentle hint of flavor is called for such as in Beurre Blanc (flavored butter) or sautéed chanterelle mushrooms.

The Cereals

What is a cereal?
Most folks think of cereal as what they pour into their bowl as breakfast. However cereal is a term that describes seeds we eat: grains (i.e. wheat, rice, corn), legumes (eg. beans, peas) and nuts.

How did cereal get its name?
The word cereal is derived from the name of the Roman goddess of agriculture, *Ceres*.

How did legumes get its name?
Legume comes from the Latin word *legre* meaning "to gather".

Is the peanut a nut?
Most people consider a peanut as a nut but it is a legume. Other legumes include chick peas, lentils, lima and soy beans.

When were cereals cultivated?
Evidence suggests that planting and harvesting cereal crops began about 8,000 years ago. There are records from 3,000 B.C. that log grain transactions. Some speculate that writing and arithmetic were developed largely to keep track of these transactions.

How is it vegetarians can get all the necessary amino acids without meat?
An amino acid is to a protein as a link is to a chain. There are 8 necessary amino acids that humans require to build the

proteins we need to survive. We primarily get these amino acids from meat. No single non-meat food has all these amino acids, so vegetarians must combine various foods to get them. For example, grains are deficient in lysine and legumes do not have sulfur-containing amino acids. However, eating grains at one meal and legumes at the next will satisfy the body's protein needs.

What different types of wheat are there?
Wheat is classified by when it is planted and the hardness of the kernel. Winter wheat is planted in the fall and remains a small plant in the winter, growing to maturity in the spring. Spring wheat is planted in the spring and reaches maturity in summer. Soft wheat, hard wheat and durum wheat are classified by the hardness of the kernel. Durum (from the Latin word *durus* meaning "hard") has the hardest kernel.

What are these various wheats best used for?
Soft wheat flour is used for cookies, cakes and pastries. Hard wheat flour is used for bread. The smaller starch grains in Durum wheat are too strong to allow the gases from yeast to rise in pockets, so Durum is not used in bread (other than in small amounts). The endosperm of Durum wheat, called Semolina, is principally used to make pasta.

What is the difference between all-purpose flour and bread flour?
All-purpose flour is a soft wheat flour with less gluten than bread flour. It works well in cakes, cookies and breads. The bread made with all-purpose flour will have a soft texture (i.e. dinner rolls) but will not rise as much bread made with bread flour. The higher levels of stretchy gluten in bread flour helps hold in the carbon dioxide gas for a higher rise.

What is bleached flour? Bromated flour?
Consumers prefer white flour to the yellow tinge of naturally milled wheat. There are two ways to remove the yellow: 1) aging flour for several months or 2) using chemicals such as benzoyl peroxide and potassium bromide. The peroxide bleaches while the bromide (hence the term bromated) artificially ages the flour. Because bleaching flour removes nutrients, it must be "enriched" by replacing some of the lost nutrients. Professional bakers report that bread made of unbleached flour allows bread to rise higher than with bleached flour.

How about cracked wheat, bran, rye and whole wheat flours?
The wheat grain has a protective coat called the "bran" and inside is the germ. Whole wheat flour is made with bran and germ whereas white flour is just the germ. Rye is often mixed with high gluten bread flour as it does not rise well on its own. Cracked wheat and bran flour are mixed with all-purpose flour in order to improve leavening.

What do barley and gladiators have in common?
Barley was the preferred grain of northern countries because of the shorter growing season. In Athens, perhaps as a testament to their hardy nature, Gladiators were called "*hordearii*" which means "barley-eaters".

Can I lose weight eating rye bread?
Rye makes a heavy bread but also has a high level of pentosans (5-carbon sugar chains). Pentosans make one feel full in two ways: they swell when ingested and they take a long time to break down into sugars. You may or may not lose weight but you will feel fuller when eating rye bread.

How long has rice been in the human diet?
Archeological evidence suggests that rice has been in the diet for more than 5,000 years. A written decree from 2,800 B.C. by a Chinese Emperor on rice planting is the first known written document about rice.

How did rice come to America?
In 1685 a Madagascar ship in need of repairs staggered into a harbor at Charles Towne, SC. To express his gratitude to the colonists who repaired his ship, the Captain gave them some "Golde Seed Rice". The rice took well in the flat, flooded and fertile soils. 15 years later, 300 tons of rice was shipped to England and thus it became both a staple and economy for the colonists.

Is growing rice good for the environment?
Rice grows best in areas that are poor for other crops or habitation. Large, flat areas that may have much clay and are frequently flooded are perfect for growing rice. The flooded rice fields are also an excellent habitat for migratory waterfowl. Additionally, the rice fields clean the water for the environment.

What is the difference between white and brown rice?
All rice begins as brown rice. White rice is milled so that the outer brown bran layer is removed. This bran layer contains oil so its shelf life is about 6 months (but longer if refrigerated). The shelf life of white rice is almost indefinite if stored in a tightly sealed container.

Does removing the bran remove vitamins?
Yes. In fact, cultures that relied heavily on rice saw a sharp rise in Beriberi when milled rice was introduced. Beriberi is caused by a deficiency in B vitamins. Today, however, white rice (called "converted rice") is naturally infused with B vitamins. Even still, it is not a good idea to wash white rice before cooking to avoid washing away some of these B vitamins. This is especially critical if the rice is to be served to children.

Is Wild Rice wild? Is it rice?
No to both questions. Wild Rice, which grew in North America around the Great Lakes region, was in the diet of

the Chippewa Indians. Today it is cultivated so it is no longer "wild". Because it is a distant relative of the rice from the Far East, it is not considered "true rice".

Is wild rice helpful to the vegetarian diet?
Wild rice is high in lysine, which is a necessary amino acid not found in most other grains.

What is Aromatic rice?
Aromatic rice (a.k.a. fragrant rice) has a natural aroma and nutty flavor. There are many types of Aromatic rice that includes Basmati, Jasmine and Texmati.

What are the differences between long, medium and short grain rice?
As you might expect, the name describes the relative length of the rice. In general, the longer the grain the less the grains stick together when cooked.

What is Arborio rice?
This medium grain rice is used in Italian risottos. It has a white dot in the center of the grain and when cooked, develops a creamy texture and a chewy center.

What is Christmas rice?
This short-grain rice is naturally red in color with an aromatic flavor. It is grown only by the Lundburg Family Farms in Richvale, CA. This farm is also the sole source for the mahogany colored Wehani rice.

How do I get rice to be more separate when cooking?
There are several methods. The easiest is to use a long grain rice. Or, add 1 teaspoon of lemon juice per cup of uncooked rice to the water before cooking. Also, one may sauté the rice

in a small amount of butter before cooking.

What is the difference between Chinese and Japanese rice vinegars?
Japanese rice vinegars are mellow whereas the Chinese vinegars are sharp and sour.

What does tossing rice at a Bride and Groom signify?
This tradition is an association of rice with fertility and that association comes from the Far East.

Corn

Where and when was corn first cultivated?
Corn was cultivated in Central America around 3500BC. Not only did the Aztecs, Incas and Mayas use the ears for food but they pressed the stalks for sugar (corn, a grass, is related to that other popular grass, sugar cane). In order to attain nutritional balance (corn is deficient in the proteins lysine and tryptophan), they also used the corn stalks as a natural trellis and planted beans along side the stalks.

Is it true that the explorer Samuel de Champlain noted in 1616 about the Huron Indians, "They have another way of eating Indian corn, to prepare which they take it in the ear and put it in water under the mud, leaving it two or three months in that state, until they judge that it is putrid; then they take it out and boil it with meat or fish and then eat it. They also roast it, and it is better this way than boiled, but I assure you nothing smells so bad as this corn when it comes out of the water all covered with mud; yet the women and children take it, suck it like sugar cane, there being nothing they like better, as they plainly show."
Yes. Yuck.

What is Maize?
Corn, to most of the world, is called maize, derived from the

Taino word "mahiz" for "grain of the gods". The Taino people were native to the Caribbean islands and introduced the grain to Columbus in 1492. The term "corn", in Middle English, means "grain" or to form into grains. When you peel back a cornhusk, you see a plethora of grains so the name appears fitting. The colonists, then, preferred to call it "Indian Corn". Unfortunately, the early colonists refused to eat maize and they nearly starved to death because of it.

Are those "baby corns" in my Asian dish real corn?
Yes. They are typically sweet corn that is picked just as it develops young kernels. Thailand is the leading producer of baby corn.

What is sweet corn?
There are dozens of types of sweet corn and it is largely grown for human consumption. Sweet corn is high in sugar with tender kernels. Fresh picked sweet corn is the best but it can also be frozen or canned.

Why does just-picked corn taste better?
Sugar corn is a hybrid corn that yields more sugar than starch but only hours after picking, much of the sugar is converted into starch. If you have ever eaten just-picked sweet corn you know it does not need cooking, butter or salt to be perfectly delicious.

What is "High-Fructose" corn syrup?
Corn does not contain syrup but it does have a lot of starch. Starch is simply a very long chain of sugars. Using natural enzymes, corn starch is broken down into fructose which is 30% sweeter than table sugar (sucrose) and handy for sweet beverages and jams.

What is succotash?
It is a dish made from corn and beans. The Native Indian name for this dish is *msikwatash,* which the Colonists pronounced as

succotash. In making succotash, lye from wood ashes is added to cut corn. The lye causes the kernel to swell and slip out of their hulls and separate from the inner germ. The name for the corn kernels, sans hulls, is hominy. Succotash is the hominy cooked with green beans and (optionally) pumpkin (or other squash). (Be sure to thoroughly wash out the lye!)

Is corn hard to grow?
It is amazing that corn ever grew on its own without human intervention. Corn cannot possibly reseed itself because the way kernels are firmly attached to the heavy cob. The kernels cannot distribute themselves yet if they grow too close together, they choke each other out. Finally, each strand of the corn's silk must trap some other corn's pollen or the kernels do not develop. The facts are, a successful corn crop depends on an order not found naturally in the randomness of nature.

What are the "Three Sisters"?
The Native American Indians named the Three Sisters as corn, beans and squash. When they planted corn, they also planted beans nearby to use the stalks as a natural trellis. Amongst the rows of corn, was planted squash. Besides being an efficient use of agricultural land, the "three sisters" provided all the nutritional amino acids necessary for a balanced diet. This was especially critical if meat (which also provides a full compliment of amino acids) was hard to come by.

What is dent corn?
When you see corn growing, it is usually dent (a.k.a. field) corn. Dent corn is identified by the dimples in the center of each kernel. It has a hard outer coat which makes for hard chewing. Primarily, dent corn is fed to livestock but is also used to make starch, corn oil and ethanol. Farmers who do plant sweet corn will often plant a few outer rows of dent corn near passing roads to discourage the less-than-scrupulous passers-

by who might try to "pick up" some very fresh corn on the ride home.

How long have humans consumed popcorn?
Excavations of Bat Caves of West Central New Mexico has revealed popcorn seeds as old as 5,600 years. Popcorn has been found in tombs on the east coast of Peru over 1,000 years old that still pop! In 1519, Cortez found that the Aztecs in Mexico wore necklaces and ceremonial headdresses of popcorn.

Was popcorn at the first Thanksgiving?
It is recorded that Quadequina, brother of Wampanoag Chief Massasoit, brought a gift of popcorn to the first Thanksgiving feast.

Why does popcorn pop and other corns do not?
Popcorn pops because of the moisture inside and the hard jacket outside. Good popcorn must have just the right amount of moisture inside to pop: 13%-14%. When the moisture is heated and turns to steam, the hard enamel "jacket" ruptures under the pressure. As the soft (gelatinized) corn starch is exposed to this high then rapidly decreasing pressure, it expands into the soft white endosperm we know as popcorn.

What is the best way to pop popcorn?
Once popped, the steam must be removed from the cooking vessel or the popcorn will re-absorb the water and become chewy and tough. A good popcorn popper must have a way for the steam to escape when the corn in popping.

Popcorn for breakfast?
In the 1700's popcorn was used as a breakfast cereal by pouring milk and sugar on top.

Mike Bellino

Ever wonder how the breakfast cereal came to be? Here's a brief history of the Breakfast Cereal Abridged from "On Food and Cooking" by Harold McGee.

A vegetarian craze in the 19th century arose in opposition to the diet of salt pork, beef, hominy and white bread. Dr. John Kellogg had this moral commentary about the diet of the day, "A man that lives on pork, fine-flour, rich pies and cakes ... drinks tea and coffee ... might well try to fly as to be chaste in thought." His voice was joined with a Presbyterian minister, Sylvester Graham, who extolled a whole grain flour which came to be known as Graham flour – and eventually led to the popular Graham Cracker.

Graham, in time, influenced Dr. James Jackson who created the first modern breakfast cereal made out of Graham flour and water, baked into a heavy bread, broken into little pieces and baked again until the small pieces were brittle. This recipe is today the basis for Post's Grape Nuts, which Dr. Jackson named "Granula".

Meanwhile, in Battle Creek, Michigan, Ellen White, a Seventh Day Adventist leader, had a "revelation" and decreed it church policy to make the human diet meatless and stimulantless. And when a sanitarium run by Graham's followers failed, the Church bought it and brought in fellow Adventist Dr. John H. Kellogg to run it.

In 1877 Dr. Kellogg, created a cereal made by cracking biscuits made from wheat, oats and corn meal. He also named his creation "Granula" but Dr. Jackson objected and Dr. Kellogg renamed it "Granola". Afterward, Dr. Kellogg temporarily lost interest in cereals and turned his attention to nuts (no, not the ones in his sanitarium) publishing a hopeful paper titled, "Nuts May Save the Race."

Then in 1893, Dr. Kellogg met Henry Perky who took the Doctor's advice to bake his shredded, freshly steamed wheat biscuits, Perky created shredded wheat, which he produced in Niagara Falls and Massachusetts.

That busy Dr. John Kellogg, was later inspired by the moderate success of "granose" (wheat flakes) and added barley malt to corn flakes. The immediate success of these corn flakes created the Battle Creek Toasted Corn Flake Company managed by Dr. Kellogg's brother, Will Keith Kellogg -- which is the W. K. Kellogg Company we know today.

Meanwhile, salesman Charles Post had spent 10 months in Dr. Kellogg's sanitarium with no change for the better. He left the sanitarium and was "cured" by a Christian Scientist and then he went on to set up his own retreat. There he made the Post Grape Nuts ("Grape" coming from the fact that the barley malt converts some of the cereal starch to glucose a.k.a. "grape sugar"). Mr. Post also went on to create the Post Toasties (first named "Elijah's Manna" but renamed after having been condemned from the pulpits) and Postum (a coffee substitute drink made out of wheat). The C. W. Post Company thrived on Charles Post's acumen for sales and marketing and was the top selling cereal brand until his death.

Finally, Alexander Anderson, working at Columbia University, accidentally shattered a hot test tube of cereal starch and noted the porous, puffy nature of the mass pouring out. Repeating his experiment on whole grains he heated them and then suddenly released the pressure and the grains puffed out. Mr. Anderson went on to join Quaker Oats in Chicago and invented the first stream-injected puffing gun. Puffed rice was introduced at the St. Louis World Fair in 1904 and found great success when it was transformed into breakfast cereal the following year.

Wine and Beer

Historical estimates place the first fermented beverages at about 10,000 years ago. As humans began to cultivate plants, the grape wine plant, Vitis vinifera, spread winemaking from the Middle East to Europe and Asia. By 700BC wine had become a staple beverage. For example, the Greek word for breakfast was *akratidzomai,* which literally meant "to drink undiluted wine". In those days, breakfast consisted of pieces of bread dipped into wine.

It seems reasonable that at some point in time, millenniums ago, yeast spoiled some picked grapes. The yeast, which consumes grape sugars, produced (excreted) alcohol. However, as the alcohol builds up in higher concentrations, it eventually kills off the yeast itself and preserves the beverage from any bacterial growth. Typically when the alcohol reached 15% of the volume, the yeast can no longer survive which is why most wines and beer contain about this level of alcohol. The ancients liked the flavor, the high calorie alcohol and loved its intoxicating properties. The fact that it didn't spoil even after years of storage added to its value.

How did the ancients consider the effects of alcohol? Pliny, for one, did not think wine was worth the effort. He wrote in his 14th book, "... so much toil and labor and expense is paid as the price of a thing that pervert's men's minds and produces madness..." Plato argues that those under 18 years of age be allowed only moderate amounts of wine until 30. He writes, "But when a man is verging on the forties, we shall tell him (to) invoke the presence of Dionysus -- I mean the wine cup -- which he bestowed on us (as) comfortable medicine against the dryness of old age, that we might renew our youth..." In more contemporary phraseology, "Party on, you old Dude!"

Is it harder to make wine or beer?
Wine is harder to make than beer because of the labor of raising, gathering and pressing the grapes. But fermenting wine is easy because the grape juice already has the sugars for the yeast. Beer (derived from the Latin word biber meaning "drink") was made from the more easily obtainable starchy grains (barley, wheat, millet, corn) and hence became the drink of the common folks as wine was the drink of the rich. In summary, it is easier to grow the beer grains but easier to ferment the wine. Let's call it a tie.

How is beer made?
The central task to making beer is to somehow breakdown the starches (complex sugars) into simple sugars for the yeast to consume. In ancient Peru this was accomplished by chewing on the grains (allowing human saliva to break down the starch) then spitting it into a pot for fermentation. Thankfully, this Bud's not for you. In modern times, brewers use malting -- the process of causing the grains to just begin to sprout -- to get the simple sugars. As the seeds sprout, the starches are converted into sugar and then the yeast can feast.

What are hops and what are they doing in my beer?
Human saliva aside, one of the most beneficial additions to beer making was hops, the resinous cones of a bine (a bine is

similar to a vine but uses downward facing hairs for stability) and is related to related Cannabis (aka Hemp). Hops are added during brewing to inhibit growth of undesired bacteria (but not the brewer's yeast), better preserves the beer and also adds the classic bitter flavor to balance the sweet malt.

How do you get beverages with high alcohol levels?
Above we learned that the natural limit for alcohol is about 15%. What if one wanted a higher concentration of alcohol in your adult beverage? Alcohol changes from liquid to gas at 173 deg F. Since (pure) water turns to steam at 212 deg F., the trick is to heat the fermented liquid such that only the alcohol leaves as a gas in a tube but then is cooled and re-condensed as liquor of higher proof then the original liquid.

My brandy says it is 80 proof. What is "proof" anyway?
If you were going to buy a potent alcoholic beverage, you'd want proof that the alcohol content was as high as expected. Thus to "Proof" a liquor, centuries ago, meant mixing it with gunpowder and igniting it. A fast burn of the mixture was proof of a higher alcohol content. Proof today is approximately twice the percentage of alcohol in a liquid. For example 100 proof means approximately 50% alcohol. The reason it is approximate is because alcohol has the unusual effect of causing water to contract. For example, mixing 53.73 parts of water to 50 parts of alcohol does not make 103.73 parts but rather 100 parts. The good news is you get (slightly) more in the bottle this way!

When cooking with alcohol, does the alcohol evaporate away?
It depends on the dish, but usually not all of the alcohol is cooked out. When measured, dishes can lose as much as 96% or as little as 51% of the alcohol. However, some of the residual liquid remains and this adds flavor to the dish. Common alcoholic beverage cooking uses: red wine in spaghetti sauce,

gravies, beef stew and marinating beef; White wine in chicken, seafood sauce, and marinating chicken or pork. Vermouth is in French Onion soup and beer is called for in chili, bread and batter.

Why do some dishes just not taste the same without alcohol?
Certainly the flavor of wine, for example, adds to the flavor of the dish, but a there's a secret to this: some flavors are drawn out not by water but by alcohol. Adding a little wine to some stewing tomatoes adds to the flavor by drawing out flavors that water could not.

What is the "head" on beer?
The white foam atop the beer is formed by the carbon dioxide in the beer being trapped by the dextrins and hop resins. Because these elements also give the beer a bitter flavor, the head can hint about the taste. Beer enthusiasts will tell you if the head of your beer reduces by half in about 2 minutes, your beer is well regarded.

I left my beer in the sun for a few hours and now it stinks!
Sunlight causes the hop resin humulone to interact with molecules containing sulfur. This reaction creates isopentenyl mercaptan – a smelly chemical similar to chemicals found in skunk's spray. This is why beer bottles are dark – to help keep the sunlight out.

How long can you store beer?
It depends on the type of beer and how it is packaged but beer is best consumed before 3-4 months have passed since it was made.

What is cork? Why is it used to plug wine bottles?
Cork is the bark of an evergreen oak native to the western Mediterranean. The cork cells are mostly air and contain a

waxy substance. These two attributes make the cork perfect for compressing into the wine bottle neck and keeping oxygen out and (in the case of champagne) carbon dioxide in.

Why keep the oxygen out of wine?
Louis Pasteur studied the effects of oxygen on wine. He correctly concluded that oxygen is necessary for winemaking but if the wine is overexposed for long periods of time, it will break down and taste poorly. The lesson: full wine bottles keep well but half empty bottles do not.

Why is champagne bubbly and clear?
Champagne, named after the Champagne wine region of France, starts out with color like all other wines. The wine is clarified by cooling and allowing the sediment to settle. Extra sugar is then added to the bottle and it's corked and kept cool (55° F) for a half-year. The yeast slowly feeds on the sugar increasing the alcohol content and creating carbon dioxide. As the bottle pressure builds, the carbon dioxide is dissolved into the wine. After several years of further aging, the bottle then cooled to 25° F is tipped down so the sediment collects in the neck. At this point, the neck is frozen and the sediment plug is  pulled out with the cork. A little wine or syrup is added (to top off the bottle) and the cork is re-inserted. With the sediment removed and the high levels of dissolved carbon dioxide, you have the clear and bubbly beverage of celebration.

Sweet Stuff...

Honey

Humans have been collecting honey for about 10,000 years and bees were "domesticated" as early as 6,000 years ago in Egypt. For almost as long, we have been associating honey with ones we love. A Sumarian tablet describes a bride's caress as "more savory than honey" and the Old Testament (Song of Songs) chants, "Thy lips, O my spouse, drop as the honeycomb: honey and milk are under thy tongue..." Which explains why the Hebrews were so eager to get to the promised land flowing of milk and honey!

What is honey made of?
The Roman author, Pliny, wrote that, "Honey comes out of the air... At early dawn the leaves of trees are found bedewed with honey..." and he goes on to wonder if honey is the sky perspiring or the saliva of the stars. Today we know that honey is really the nectar that bees collect from flowers. Honey is up to 80% sugar (glucose, fructose and/or sucrose depending on the type of flowers the bees visit) and more than 200 other substances including (surprisingly) trace amounts of glutamic acid (MSG) and phenylalanine (also found in the artificial sweetener aspertame).

What do the bees do with the nectar they drink up?
The bees have a sac for storing the nectar. In this sac it is mixed with enzymes to break down whatever starches there are into sugars.

What happens when the bees return to the hive?
Once in the hive, the bees pump the nectar in and out of themselves for 15 to 20 minutes (to reduce the water content) then deposit it into the comb. To further reduce the water content the bees fan the honey with their wings until the water content is about 20%. The main reason for the evaporation is to preserve the honey. As it is now hygroscopic (water absorbing), it fends off yeasts and other microbes that would otherwise ferment the honey into alcohol.

How far do the bees have to fly to make 1 lb of honey?
As they fly back and forth to the hive, the bees cover the equivalent of 3 orbits about the earth to make 1 lb of honey. In case you are wondering, a bee gets about 7,000,000 miles to a gallon of honey.

Can honey be different colors?
Honey color ranges from almost clear to various shades of amber to even black. The more clear the honey, the more mild the taste. The dark honey contains more minerals (8 times the potassium) and nitrogen.

My honey becomes lumpy or granulated. What's happening?
Granulated honey indicates the honey is cold or has lost too much water. Since granulation is also dependent on the type of honey, two different jars stored in the same place may show granulation in one and not the other. Granulated honey is prone to fermentation so gently heat the honey and add a very small amount of water to restore the honey to its stable liquid state.

Is honey antiseptic?
Honey has been uses for thousands or year to treat wounds due to its antibacterial properties. Honey is hygroscope (absorbs water), acidic and with a small amount of water added, forms hydrogen peroxide. All these characteristics are ideal for slowing or stopping infections.

Can honey be poisonous?
Some plants yield nectar that is fine for bees but toxic to humans. These plants include azaleas, mountain laurels and rhododendrons. Around 400BC a Greek army under Xenophon was decimated simply for having fed upon "mad honey" made from Rhododendrons.

Is honey safe for children?
Although very rare, honey may contain *Clostridium botulinum* spores that can cause infant botulism. Keep honey away from children under 1 year of age. It is possible to pasteurize the honey to kill these spores.

Honey Tip: You can substitute honey in a recipe normally calling for sugar (1 part honey to 1.25 parts sugar). You will have to slightly decrease the amount of water added since honey contains more water than table sugar. But because honey is more hygroscopic than table sugar it will keep cakes and breads moister longer holding onto the moisture and even re-absorbing moisture on humid days.

Sugar

Sugar cane is a 20 foot tall grass which originated in the South Pacific and spread to Asia. The plant is harvested and pressed to extract the sweet juice inside. The juice, containing about 13% sucrose, is processed to extract the sugar.

Is raw sugar unprocessed?
Raw sugar is processed but the processing is minimal. Eating completely unprocessed sugar is neither healthy nor palatable due to the parasites you are sharing the sugar with.

Mike Bellino

How is white sugar made?
Today, extracting white sugar is a repetition of boiling down
the juice, allowing crystallization and separating out the
molasses syrup with a centrifuge until white sugar remains.
In the pre-centrifuge days, the reduced liquid was poured into
rounded cone-shaped clay molds. As the sugar crystallized, the
molasses and extra water would drip out a small hole in the
bottom of the mold. After a week and a half, the now solid
block of sugar crystal is turned over and removed from the
mold. The rounded cones of sugar were called sugarloaves.

How did the "sugarloaf" mountains get their name?
Due to the physical similarity to the rounded cones of sugar.

What are the grades of molasses?
The first molasses is light and sweet. It is sometimes served as
syrup. The second molasses is darker and is typically use for
cooking and baking. The third molasses – blackstrap molasses
- is bitter and dark.

Why does my molasses say "unsulphured"?
Long ago molasses was treated with sulfur dioxide to lighten
the color and kill molds and bacteria. Unfortunately sulfur
dioxide is offensive to the olfactory sense so molasses producers
have found other ways.

How are sugar cubes made?
The original sugar cube patent was issued to the Swiss Jakub
Krystof Rad in 1843. Back then, sugar came in hard loaves
and were hard to break up. Mr. Rad invented a device that cut
the loaves into small cube shapes called "tea sugar". Today,
water is added to sugar and then it is simply poured into cube-
shaped molds. The water is dried out and the cube is naturally
formed.

What is brown sugar? Can I use white sugar for brown sugar?
Originally brown sugar was processed sugar but still retained its original molasses. Today, a number of sugar manufactures actually spray molasses on white sugar rather than stop at the "brown sugar" phase of sugaring. If you run out of brown sugar you can substitute a mixture of white sugar and molasses. To substitute for dark brown sugar, add 2 tablespoons of molasses for each cup of white sugar. For light brown sugar, add just 1 tablespoon per cup of white sugar.

Brown sugar tips: When a recipe calls out for brown sugar, it is assumed the sugar is to be packed for measuring (unless specifically stated otherwise). Hard lumps in brown sugar can be softened by placing a damp paper towel in the container for several days. The sugar will absorb the water and soften.

What is Turbinado sugar?
This is raw sugar that has undergone minimal process to wash out the microbes and other contaminants present in the sugar cane. It is similar to light brown sugar in composition.

What is beet sugar?
Partly due to protests against the use of slaves in the sugar fields (and other political reasons), a demand grew for sugar not made from imported cane. In 1747, the Prussian chemist, Andreas Marggraf invented a method for extracting sugar from beets which is indistinguishable from refined cane sugar. However, the average white beet yields only 1 to 4% sugar. German scientists, in the late 18th century, successfully bred the sugar beet which contains 15-20% sugar. Today, more than 250 million tons of sugar beet sugar is produced world wide.

How do I know if the sugar I buy is beet sugar or cane sugar?
Check the label. If it says "pure cane sugar" then it is. If it

does not, it is likely beet sugar. Once refined, the two sugars chemically identical and can be used in the same manner.

What is "sorghum"?
Sorghum is a tall grass which has a sweet pith. The pith can be boiled down to sorghum syrup.

What is maple syrup?
Maple Syrup is essentially tree sap. In the same way that honey is reduced from nectar and sugar is reduced from cane or beet juice, maple syrup is reduced from the tree sap of certain varieties of maple trees. Of the maple species, the *Acer saccharum* maple affords the best quality and quantity sap.

Why does the maple sap run?
All summer long the maple tree, through photosynthesis, creates sugar in the leaves and stores it in the sapwood (inner layers) of the trunk. As the spring daytime temperatures begin to rise above the freezing mark, the carbon dioxide gas trapped in the sap is released and builds pressure in the sapwood forcing the sap outwards. Additionally, sugar induced osmotic pressure contributes to the pressure buildup. When the nighttime temperatures return to freezing, a suction is created which draws in water from the roots. In the early spring this process repeats daily and the sap runs. When the nighttime temperatures no longer fall below freezing, the sap stops running.

How much sap does it take to make a gallon of maple syrup?
35 to 40 gallons of sap are typically required to make one gallon of pure maple syrup.

Where does the maple syrup color come from?
Maple sap, as it runs from the tree, is a slightly sweet, clear liquid. It contains about 2% to 10% sugar. The maple syrup

color is a result of the browning reaction that occurs near the end of evaporation. The longer the sap is boiled, the darker colored the syrup.

When is boiled maple sap, syrup?
Maple syrup is boiled to 7°F (3.9°C) above the boiling point of water at your location. Since the boiling point of water changes with altitude and atmospheric pressure, it is best to take the temperature of boiling water when your sap is close to the syrup stage. Using the recently acquired boiling point, add 7°F (3.9°C) to that value. This is the finishing temperature for your syrup.

Are there any preservatives in maple syrup?
Maple syrup does not have any preservatives thus, after opening, should be refrigerated. In the refrigerator, the shelf-life is about six months.

What is the best container to buy maple syrup in?
Plastic containers allow some gas exchange that will degrade the syrup after 3 to 6 months of storage. Glass retains the quality longer than plastic. The traditional tin container is better than plastic but not good as glass. Whatever you choose, if you use the syrup in a few months, it does not much matter.

Can maple syrup be used in place of white sugar?
Yes. For baking or cooking, use ¾ cup maple syrup for each cup of white sugar. If you are baking, additionally reduce the total liquid in the recipe by 3 Tablespoons for each cup of syrup used.

Can syrup be made from other trees as well?
Birch syrup can be made from birch trees and has a distinctly different taste from maple syrup. Compared to Maple, Birch sap runs for half the time, has half the sugar content and due to

different sugar types, is easier to burn when boiling down. For these reasons, it is much more expensive than maple syrup.

Substitute sugar

What are the differences between the various low calorie sugar substitutes?
At this writing, there are four types of sugar substitutes: saccharin (a.k.a. Sweet-n-low), Acesulfame potassium (a.k.a. Sunett and Sweet One), Aspertame (a.k.a. Equal, Nutrasweet), sucralose (a.k.a. Splenda) and neotame.

Saccharin is an organic chemical that tastes 300 times as sweet as sugar. However, since it is indigestible, we get no calories from it. Since 1977, Saccharin was a suspected cancer causing agent. However, by 2001 the US department of Health and Human Services was unable to find a substantial link between Saccharin and cancer so the warning labels were repealed. You can use saccharin in baking, but you still need to add sugar to get acceptable volume and moistness. This allows you reduce the sugar, and hence the calories, but retains the sweetness.

Acesulfame potassium is about 200 times sweeter the sucrose. It is chemically similar to Saccharin.

Aspertame is a protein that is about 200 times sweeter than sugar. Because it is a protein, it is digested by the body. However, since a very small amount is needed for sweetening, it adds very little to your caloric intake.

Why did my diet soda from the basement storage taste so bad?
Aspertame, in diet soda, breaks down over time so it limits the shelf life to about 3 months. It sat in your basement too long!

Can I bake with Aspertame?
Aspertame does not work well for baking because the heat causes the protein to lose some of its sweetness.

Why can't some people drink diet drinks sweetened with Aspertame?
There exists a small population of people who have the genetic disease phenylketonuria (PKU) who lack the enzyme to break down the amino acid phenylalanine contained in Aspertame. Afflicted people need to monitor their intake of phenylalanine. All children in the U.S.A. are tested for PKU at birth.

Is Neotame the same as Aspertame?
Both sweeteners are made by the Nutrasweet company. Neotame could be considered the next generation Aspertame. Unlike Aspertame, it can be used in baked goods and does not require a special labeling for phenylketonuric individuals (though it does contain phenylalanine).

Sucralose is modified cane sugar. Three of the hydrogen-oxygen groups in the sugar (sucrose) are replaced with chlorine atoms. This makes the resulting sucralose molecule 600 times sweeter than sugar and indigestible. It also does not break down in heat so it can be used in baking recipes.

What is sorbitol?
Found in "sugar free" candies, Sorbitol is a naturally occurring sweet alcohol. It may be sugar free (good for diabetics), but it is not calorie free.

Ice Cream

What is ice cream?
Ice cream is essentially frozen milk foam. In addition to frozen foam (air whipped into frozen milk), it also contains some liquid and ice crystals.

Where did ice cream get its start?

The French, who were fond of the frozen treat "fruit ice", are the first on record to have served "cream ice" in the 17th century.

Who invented the ice cream maker?

The American Nancy Johnson invented the hand-crank ice cream maker in 1846. There are two key points to making ice cream. 1) bringing the sweet milk mixture to below freezing temperatures and 2) whipping air into the mixture as it cools. Ms. Johnson's invention used ice and salt to bring the temperatures below freezing and incorporated a multi-blade mixer to whip in the air. Unfortunately for Ms. Johnson, in America, patent rights are to those who are first to file, not first to invent. Two years after Ms. Johnson's invention, William G. Young patented the ice cream maker.

Why does ice cream need air whipped into it?

Whipping air into ice cream is called "overrun". If no air were added, the ice cream would be very hard to scoop and eat. Most commercial ice creams are 50% air, while premium ice creams are about 20% air.

How did the ice cream sundae get its name?

In 1875, the town of Evanston, IL decided that shops serving ice cream sodas on Sunday led to frivolity unbecoming of good Sunday behavior. The town passed an ordinance prohibiting ice cream sodas sales on Sunday. The Drug Store owners circumvented the law by serving ice cream without the soda but with the syrup of your choice. The shopkeepers felt guilty naming this treat served on Sunday as "sunday" so the spelling was changed to "sundae".

What are the optimum temperatures for ice cream?
Store ice cream between –10 and 0 deg F. Repeated thawing and freezing can cause ice crystals to form. Serve at 10 deg F.

Vitamins

Perhaps because Americans have such a strong sense of control over their lives, nutrition has fallen pray to a number of fads. It is my personal observation, having read clips from older books, that much of the nutritional information dispensed today is simply recycled from generations previous. Often, modern society continues to believe these recycled myths. However today we at least have more comprehensive research to understand the chemistry behind the nutrition. In prior generations, the nutritionists were largely guessing.

Just as well, food has to be nutritious as well as tasty in order to sustain good health. With this in mind we will examine some fun food facts about vitamins.

How did vitamins get their names?
Vitamin is a contraction of "vital amine" although vitamins were later discovered not to be amines at all. Vitamins are "vital" substances that the body needs to function, but does not create on its own. It needs to gather vitamins from other sources such as plants, animals, and bacteria.

Vitamin A and B was arbitrarily named because A was fat soluble and B is water soluble. Vitamin C derived from "ascorbic". No special reasons for D and E, but K was named by a Danish scientist who noted that K caused blood coagulation (or koagulation as it was spelled).

Vitamin C: Linus Pauling, the Noble Prize winning Chemist, argued that ample levels of Vitamin C would rid the world of the Common Cold if only we all took 2.3 grams (40 times the required amount). Additionally he suggested Vitamin C would eliminate Heart Disease and Cancer. Today his writings have made Vitamin C a staple for treating colds but there is little clinical evidence to support its effectiveness.

Vitamin A: Also known as "Retinol", because it is vital for the workings of the eye, Vitamin A can be found in green and yellow vegetables, milk, butter, cheese, egg, yolk, and liver. Orange vegetables (eg. carrots) and dark green vegetables contain the highest levels of Vitamin A and carotenoids (which is a precursor to Vitamin A). Vitamin A, while necessary, is poisonous in large quantities. For example, in 1974, an 48-year old Briton drank a gallon of carrot juice each day to demonstrate the health benefits of Vitamin A. After 10 days of his nutritional regiment, he died of severe liver damage -- his skin was bright yellow.

Vitamin K: It is not made by animals but by the bacteria which inhabit their (our) intestines. We feed the bacteria with the food we eat and the bacteria return the favor by creating Vitamin K.

Thiamine: It prevents Beriberi (Sri Lanka word for "weakness") and helps the chemical machinery, which converts food into energy. It is found in many meats, peanuts and unwashed rice.

Niacin (Vitamin B3): Originally called Nicotinic Acid but had its name shorted to avoid confusion with the tobacco drug nicotine. In fact, bread fortified with Niacin (then called Nicotinic Acid) scared the anti-tobacco crowd into thinking the bread could induce an addition to cigarettes. Niacin helps cells maintain healthy metabolism and repair DNA.

Mike Bellino

Cobalamin (Vitamin B12): This DNA precursor is critical for bone marrow and red blood cell production. Strict vegetarians can damage the digestive tract and spinal cord due to Cobalamin deficiencies. Eggs or other diary products in the diet will avoid this problem.

Tidbits & Morsels

Why do we need to refrigerated eggs from the supermarket?
When a hen lays eggs, she typically lays one egg per day in the nest. She does not sit on the nest until she considers there be a sufficient number of eggs. A clutch of eggs can be somewhere around 6 to 12 eggs.

Since the first eggs are not sat on for a week or two, they need to be protected from the outside bacterial world. When a hen lays an egg, a thin liquid coats the eggshell as it leaves the hen. This coating dries quickly (in seconds or minutes) and protects the egg from bacteria.

None of the eggs, if fertilized, actually start to develop until the hen sits on the egg, warming them, for a long time (said to be when a hen gets "broody"). In this way, the eggs will all develop and hatch together.

Eggs, as we have learned, must be not go bad for at least two weeks, and the protective coating ensures this. However, eggs purchased at the supermarket are washed, which removes the coating. These eggs need to be refrigerated. They may also be waxed to prevent moisture loss.

If you purchase eggs from a local farmer, and they are not washed, you may store them at room temperature for up to two weeks. However, it is recommended that you give the eggs as quick rinse before you crack or cook them to reduce the chance of contamination.

Mike Bellino

How do I tell if an egg is fresh or not?
Put the egg in a bowl of tap water. If the egg sinks, it is fresh; if one end floats up, it is OK to eat but not fresh. Should the egg float then it is rotten. This test works because the air inside the shell increases as the egg ages causing the egg to float.

Are egg yolks with red spots on them OK to eat?
In short, yes. Occasionally, as the egg is formed in the hen, blood vessels may rupture leaving small flecks of red in the yolk. Usually these eggs are sorted out when graded but are safe to eat.

Is there any nutritional or taste difference between white and brown eggs?
The color of the egg shell does not indicate the taste or nutritional value of the egg. The only difference is the breed of the chicken –- some lay white eggs, some lay brown. The biggest difference between eggs has more to do with the freshness of the eggs and what the hens are fed.

Is it true that some eggs can have green or blue eggshells?
There are some breeds of hens that lay eggs with green shells. Other breeds (eg. Araucana & Ameraucana breeds) lay blue-green eggs. Some breeds (eg. Maran, Welsummer) even lay eggs with colored speckles on them!

What is Filé powder?
This powder is ground up leaves of the sassafras tree. It is commonly used in gumbo where it adds a kick to the flavor and thickens the base as well.

What is the Holy Trinity?
Religion aside, the Holy Trinity is three commonly used ingredients which underscore an ethnic family of dishes. The three distinct ingredients blend together to make a common

flavor. There are many examples, here are several:

> French (Mirepoix) trinity: celery, onions, carrots
> Cajan Trinity: bell pepper, celery, onion
> Italian (Soffritto) trinity: tomato, onion, garlic
> Mexican trinity: beans, corn, chilies
> Chinese trinity: garlic, scallions, ginger

What is the odd hat that chefs wear?
It is called a toque, which is derived from the Old Spanish word *toca* meaning headdress. Headwear for cooks was implemented for sanitary reasons but they came to distinguish the master chefs. Originally the brimless toque blanche (white cap) was flat but later, height was added to provide a little cooling for the chef working under hot conditions.

What is a calorie?
A calorie is a unit of energy. Specifically, a calorie is the energy required to heat one gram of water one degree centigrade. However, this is not what a nutritional calorie is. See below.

OK, so what is a nutritional calorie?
As you can imagine, it does not take a great deal of energy to heat 1 gram of water 1 degree C when compared to our human bodies which weigh, say, 70,000 grams. Nutritionists, who talk in terms of thousands of calories, have abbreviated a kilocalorie (1,000 calories) as one nutritional calorie. Thus, a can of soda that contains 150 nutritional calories actually contains 150,000 calories. Those 150,000 calories (theoretically) will raise the temperature of 10,000 grams of water 15 degrees C.

What is the beer diet?
During one memorable high-school physics class, we learned about calories. Our instructor (Mr. White) challenged us to calculate how many calories our bodies expend when we

drink a cold beer (34° F) and warm it up to body temperature (about 99° F). We then compared the expended calories to the calories on the beer can and learned that drinking cold beer would expend more calories than were ingested and hence, weight would be lost. When this conclusion was realized, the room was silent. The students (especially guys) sat in rapt attention. Could it be true? Could drinking beer bring on slimmer bodies?

The truth is, as discussed above, that nutritional calories are 1,000 times (kilocalories) the calories calculated and hence, the beer diet utopia evaporated quickly.

Where did the ice cream cone come from?
There are many who claim to have invented the first ice cream cone, but there has not been consensus on a single claim. What is known is that in the early 1800's there is evidence to ice cream cones having been used.

What's this I hear about making a Meringue in a copper bowl?
It is a culinary tradition to use a copper pot and copper utensils when making meringue. The centuries old claim is that the meringue will be harder to ruin when made in copper bowls. Today, evidence supports this claim having found that a reaction between the copper ions and the egg whites makes it hard to overbeat the meringue. On the other hand, it does turn the meringue from snowy white to slightly yellow. If you do not have copper bowls and utensils on hand, try using a little bit of cream of tartar.

What does Cream of Tartar do for egg whites?
When whipping egg whites, the whipping action causes strands of egg proteins (albumin) to "unfurl" and interconnect with other protein strands, trapping in air and increasing in volume. Adding Cream of Tartar increases the proteins' ability to stick

together. The results are fluffier whipped egg whites with more stability (won't collapse).

Why do we taste and how does it work?
Chefs fret about a dish's aesthetic appearance, texture and smell but it is good taste that primarily discriminates the good dish from the bad.

Even the simplest creatures have some form of taste. Protozoa are wired to move toward sugar and away from poisonous alkaloids. By baring nerve endings to the ocean water, aquatic animals can seek the good food and avoid the bad. Taste has become an efficient way to find food and avoid poisons for all creatures.

Humans have several thousand taste buds that populate our tongue. Infants have many more taste buds that are not only on the top of the tongue, but on the bottom and the back of the throat. This explains why children are more sensitive to strong spices/flavors and tend to prefer what we adults consider as bland foods. Adults gradually lose taste buds, especially after the age of 45.

Taste buds, which have a lifetime of about 10 days, are a collection of sensory cells, which form in small papillae (Latin for "nipple"). Ironically, most of the taste buds, in the middle of the tongue, do not taste anything. However taste buds around the edge of the tongue detect the flavors of sweet, sour, bitter, salty. The taste buds detect taste via an exchange of molecular ions between the food and proteins on the surface of the taste bud. As the ions penetrate the membrane, small electrical signals are generated and are transmitted to the brain. The brain, in turn, maps the nerve's signals to flavors.

Various chemical structures can create or inhibit tastes that are other than the basic four. MSG (Monosodium glutamate), for example, accentuates the salty and bitter tastes. On the other hand, a compound found in artichokes (cynarin) blocks all other receptors other than sweet. Try eating an artichoke heart some time then eat anything immediately after; you will taste only sweet. Artificial sweeteners such as Saccharin and Aspartame also fool the taste buds into thinking high energy sugar is stomach bound, but in fact Saccarin cannot be digested and Asparatame, a protein, offers virtually no calories because of the small amount consumed.

What is MSG?
MSG (Monosodium glutamate) is a naturally occurring salt. It is found naturally in mushrooms, seaweed, parmesan cheese and tomatoes. A Japanese scientist first isolated the salt in kombu seaweed and named it *aji-no-moto* which means "essence of taste". It is not known quite why MSG brings out the flavor in food. One theory is the MSG makes certain food molecules stick longer to the tongue's receptors, which yields more intense flavor. It is also possible to make MSG by fermenting wheat under certain conditions (eg. soy sauce).

Is MSG bad for me?
In small amounts, usually not. If you consume a lot of MSG laden food quickly on an empty stomach, you may suffer from the so-called "Chinese restaurant syndrome" and experience pains or burning in the chest and pressure behind the eyes and forehead. There does not appear to be conclusive research linking MSG ingestion with "Chinese restaurant syndrome". Note that a "No MSG" label does not guarantee any free glutamates. If you are sensitive to MSG, stay away from foods containing "hydrolyzed protein" as well.

Can MSG reduce sodium in a diet?
If you are on a reduced sodium diet, you may consider using MSG to flavor your foods. MSG has about 1/3 the sodium of

table salt and can sufficiently flavor food with about half the added sodium.

Why does starch thicken sauces?
Starch is a complex carbohydrate – that is to say a chain of sugar molecules. It has the property of swelling into a gel when heated in a liquid. It also has the unfortunate property of forming lumps if the powder is added directly to hot liquid! The seed-based starches; wheat flour and corn starch. The root starches; arrowroot, potato starch and tapioca. The wheat and corn starches gel at about 145°F (65°C) but the root starches gel at lower temperatures.

Starch tip: When adding starch, make sure the liquid is cool. If you have a hot liquid that requires more thickening, add the starch to a cool liquid (i.e. 1 tablespoon of corn starch to 1 tablespoon of water) and stir completely. Then pour slowly into the hot liquid while whisking. Some recipes call from working starch into softened butter or margarine, which prevents lumps as well.

Why are some starches cooked in fat before adding a liquid?
The seed starches (wheat, corn) impart a cereal taste to the sauce. Cooking them in fat before adding the liquid diminishes this undesirable artifact. Starch cooked in fat/oil is called a *roux*.

What advantages do root starches have?
Root starches (potato, arrowroot, tapioca) do not impart a cereal taste to the sauce and gel at lower temperatures that makes them good for lower temperature egg-based foods such as custards and puddings.

We eat rocks?
Halite, more commonly know as rock salt, is the only natural rock we eat. Too much salt is deadly but so is no salt – we need salt to survive. The Latin name for salt (*sal*) was derived

from the Latin name for *salus*, meaning health. Rock salt was so valued in Roman times that Roman soldiers were paid, in part, for their services in salt. Payment for services in salt became known as a salary and gave rise to the saying, "worth his salt".

Why does most salt have iodine added?
Although seawater contains both salt and iodine, salt does not naturally contain iodine. A hundredth of a percent of iodine is added to salt to prevent afflictions such as goiter. Some believe the iodine in salt, when used in baking, imparts an acrid taste to the baked goods so they use salt without iodine.

Red, black, gray and pink salts?
Salts from around the globe are collected and often clay, algae or even lava of various colors are included. These natural additives do affect the flavor of the salt.

Is Sea Salt always from the sea?
Due to legal loopholes, it does not have to be from the sea and sometimes it is not.

What is Kosher Salt?
Kosher salt is course grains of salt used in the Koshering process of preserving meat. The irregular shape of the salt grains allows it to adhere better to raw meat.

What is the difference between baking powder and baking soda?
Both are used to leaven baked goods. Baking soda is used in recipes that also call for an acid (i.e. lemon juice, buttermilk). When the acid is added, the baking soda and acid react making bubbles that cause the food to rise. If the recipe does not call for acid, then baking powder is used. Baking powder is baking soda combined with a dry acid. When baking powder gets wet, the soda and acid combine to make the leavening bubbles.

What is double-acting baking powder?
Ideally one wants the leavening bubbles to develop during baking so they are better trapped by firming batter. Double-acting baking powder is treated so that much of the bubble production occurs when the powder is heated yielding lighter baked goods.

Who is Rumford and why is there a baking powder named after him?
Lord Rumford was an amateur scientist, Bavarian War Minister and American cooking enthusiast. But he never made baking powder. Rumford's endowment to Professors who showed exceptional achievements in Science and Cooking apparently earned the respect of Rumford Co. co-founder Eben Horsford who named his patented baking powder after Count Rumford in 1859.

What is Sour Salt?
Also known as Lemon Salt, it is not a salt but an acid: Citric Acid. It is often used to add a tart flavor to various foods.

Is Pure Vanilla extract the same as Imitation Vanilla?
Synthetic vanillin is identical to real vanillin. However, there are more than 100 additional compounds in real Vanilla that yields a more complex flavor than the less expensive imitation. Do not store vanilla extract in the fridge. Its flavor will actually improve with age (to a point, of course) and can be stored up to 4 years.

I bought some vanilla beans. How do I store then?
Keep them in an airtight bag in the refrigerator. They will keep for 6 months. Should the beans dry out, add one apple wedge to the bag for every two beans and seal for four days.

Caramelized onions, chewy caramel… What is caramelizing?
When sugar is heated above 365° F, it progresses from colorless to yellow to various shades of brown and eventually black.

(Think of roasting marshmallows over a fire.) Caramelization is the process of heating sugar to a shade of brown. The chemical reactions that occur cause the sweet sugar to develop a slightly bitter, cooked flavor. Caramel candies and peanut brittle, for example, benefit from this effect. It may not seem obvious, but onions hold more sugar (in the form of starch) than one might expect. When onions are heated in an oil or fat, the sugars within caramelized and violà, you have caramelized onions.

Does caramelization cause meats to turn brown?
Although there are some sugars in meat that contributes to the browning, the browning of meat in high heat is a chemical reaction known as the Maillard reaction. It is this effect which gives grilled and roasted meats their savory flavor.

What makes for better grilling: Gas or Charcoal?
Gas (propane) grilling is more convenient, other than that, it plays second fiddle to charcoal. There are essentially two reasons to grill: 1) to cook meat quickly so as to keep the meat moist as possible. 2) to cook the meat long and slow and, in the process, impart a smoke flavor into the meat while tenderizing the meat.

In case #1, charcoal gets upwards of about 700ºF while gas tops off about 500ºF. These extra 200ºF means that meat cooks faster, which in turn means there is less time to lose moisture. Also the higher heat causes more of the savory Maillard reaction (browning) on the outside of the meat. This works best with tender, thin sliced (typically 1 inch or less) cuts of meat.

In case #2, slowly roasting tougher cuts with long, slow heat breaks down the tough collagen (muscle interconnect) into gelatin and infuses a smoked flavor to the meat. When the meat is sliced, after many hours roasting over low heat and smoke, you will notice a pink ring around the outer edge of the slice – the smoke turned the meat pink.

So, while the gas grill is easier, the charcoal grill delivers a better culinary experience.

Why should I not put acidic dishes in contact with aluminum?

Aluminum is dissolved by acids and this can impart a metal taste to the food. If you put aluminum foil over (for example) lasagna in a metal dish, the two different metals combine with the acid to create a battery. The chemical reaction in this "kitchen battery" will eat away (oxidize) the foil leaving little holes wherever there was contact between the foil and the acidic food. (One remedy is to put the acidic food in a glass container.)

What is vinegar?

The name vinegar derives from the French words *vin aigre* which translates to sour wine. That is pretty much what vinegar is – a fermenting liquid which ferments too far. In fermentation, yeast or bacteria turns sugar into ethyl alcohol. Vinegar is created when the bacteria *Acetobacter aceti* converts ethyl alcohol into sour acetic acid.

We drink Lithium?

In the 1940's, there was a beverage with added lithium known as "Lithiated Lemon-Lime Soda" which advertised its ability to add "an abundance of energy, enthusiasm, a clear complexion and shining eyes." Today we know this soda as 7-Up. The reason for the claims pertains to Lithium's medical benefits as a primary treatment for manic depression and that it is also effective in treating aggression, alcoholism, epilepsy, and schizophrenia. Additionally, Lithium is anti-bacterial and is the primary chemical in the various types of Lithium batteries.

Bibliography - Recommended Reading

Below are a collection of books I own which I find interesting, unique, and even critical for cooking references.

Books #1 & #2:
"On Food and Cooking" by Harold McGee. Published by Simon & Schuster, 1988. ISBN: 0-684-84328-5

"The Curious Cook" by Harold McGee. Published by North Point Press, 1990. ISBN 0-86547-452-4

Both these books are excellent references for the hard-core food aficionados. "On Food and Cooking" is almost 700 pages of deep details on the origins, uses, and scientific explanations of all things edible. The author, Harold McGee, deserves every accolade he has received for this ground breaking book.

"The Curious Cook" is a more focused, pragmatic book that contemplates experiments and seeks to understand several food and cooking quandaries. Mr. McGee's background as a chemist is critical to the success of this book.

"What Einstein Told His Cook" by Robert L. Wolke. Published by W. W. Norton & Company, 2002. ISBN: 0-393-01186-6

Robert Wolke has a gift for taking complex science and explaining it in everyday terms. The book not only covers food, but cooking techniques and tools as well. Like Mr. McGee above, Mr. Wolke also is a chemist by training.

"I'm Just Here For the Food" by Alton Brown. Published by Stewart, Tabori & Chang, 2002. ISBN: 1-58479-083-0

Alton Brown is better known for his fun, entertaining and, ultimately, educational TV show "Good Eats" on Food Network. Mr. Brown's book, "I'm Just Here For the Food" is really an extension of his TV show as it entertains and explains in an illustrative manner not found in any other book that I know of.

"The Joy of Cooking" by Irma S. Rombauer and Marion Rombauer Becker. Published by Macmillan, 1975. ISBN: 0-02-604570-2

This book was given to Mary & I as a wedding gift. I'm sure the givers of this gift thought that Mary was going to read this book from cover to cover. Ha!

"The Joy of Cooking" is a classic and really ought to be in every cookbook collection. In more than 900 pages, the authors cover just about every imaginable type and style of cooking with accompanying recipes. There are even recipes for squirrel, opossum and porcupine, just in case, I guess, you hit one on the road. To be prepared for anything, have this book in your collection.

"The Pharaoh's Feast" by Oswald Rivera. Published by Four Walls Eight Windows, 2003. ISBN: 1-56858-282-X

I had the great pleasure of meeting Mr. Rivera in 2004. His book takes you on a tour of food over the ages from the "Beginning" to modern times. The book has recipes, to be sure, but is heavily laden with fascinating history and sometimes explains the effect of history on food, or conversely, food on history. To name a few stops along the historical path, there's the Pharaohs, Roman times, Medieval Europe, Arab world, Chinese Kingdoms, and even American fare.

"Morton Salt Home Meat Curing Guide", published by Morton Salt, Chicago, IL, 60606-1743.

If you want to learn how to process your own hams, bacon and do it safely, this is an excellent booklet to start with. Morton Salt is a reputable source and they take you step by step through the process. You are limited to curing products made by Morton Salt, but as I said, this is a great starting point if you want to learn to do it safely.

"Bull Cook and Authentic Historical Recipes and Practices" by George L. Herter and Berthe E. Herter. This book was printed by Herter's, Inc. (Waseca, MN) as late as 1964, but is currently out of print.

If ever there was a cookbook cult classic, this is it! "Bull Cook" is the ultimate in Americana people, places, food, recipes and techniques. It is a very entertaining read – you feel like you're listing to Grandpa tell you everything he ever knew about the world. I'm not certain I'd take everything Mr. Herter said as gospel truth, but there is no question he knew a very great deal about what he speaks. As I said, this book is out of print, but if you can get your hands on it, you will find it well worth the effort!

Index

A

alcohol 70
  proof 72
alkaloids 27
artichoke 23, 94
artificial sweeteners 82
avacado 26

B

baking powder 96
  double acting 97
baking soda 96
barley 61
beans 29
beer 71
  head 73
  hops 72
  making 71
  stink 73
bread 33
  dough 34
  kneading 34
  sourdough 35
butter 2, 6, 7
  clarified 7
  dry 7
  European 7
  ghee 7
  sweet 6
buttermilk 6, 7, 10

C

calorie 91
  beer diet 91
  nutritional 91
carob 54
  carats 55
carrot 1
ceral
  breakfast 68
  corn flakes 69
  granola 68
  grape nuts 69
  puffed rice 69
  shredded wheat 69
cereal 59
  history 59
champagne 74
cheese 2, 9, 10
  Brie 10
  Camembert 10
  cheddar 11
  cottage 10
  mysost 9
  raw milk 11
  ricotta 9
  roquefort 11
  spider 11
  Swiss 10
  The feet of God 10
chef hat 91
chocolate 52

alternative 54
bittersweet 54
caffeine 52
Chiapa Real 52
Dutch 54
milk chocolate 54
pets 53
white 54
coffee
  arabica 48
  brewing 47
  caffeine 48
  kopi luwak 49
  legend 47
  robusta 48
corn 64
  baby 65
  dent 66
  history 64
  popcorn 67
  sweet 65
  syrup 65
cream 5, 6
  heavy 5
  light 5
  whipping 5
crustaceans 43
cyanide 28

E

egg
  eggshell color 90
  refrigeration 89
  test 90

F

filé powder 90
flour 60
  bleached 61
  bromated 61
  whole wheat 61
fruit 15
  apple 15, 17
  apple cider 17
  apple juice 17
  banana 15, 16, 17
  cranberries 19
  false 19
  fig 16
  grapefruit 18
  Kiwi fruit 20
  orange 15, 18
  pear 16, 17
  pineapple 16, 19, 20
  seeds 28
  stone 18
  storage 17
  strawberry 15
  vegetables 15
  watermelon 15, 19

G

galic
  body odor 58
garlic
  health 58
  odor 57
  slang 57
goitrins 29
grilling 98

H

holy trinity 90
honey 75
  colors 76
  history 75

making 76
  toxic 77
hot pepper
  capsaicin 25
  Scoville scale 25

I

ice cream 83
  cone 92
  maker 84
  sundae 84

L

lactase 4
lactose 4
lard 40
lemon juice 7
LSD 27

M

Maillard reaction 98
maize. *See* corn
maple syrup 80
  color 80
  containers 81
margarine 7
meat 36
  beef 36, 37
  before refrigeration 40
  brine 41
  capon 38
  chicken 36, 38
  cooking temperature 39
  dark meat 38
  fish 36, 42
  kosher 37
  lamb 36
  myoglobin 37

pork 36
resting meat 39
safety 40
slaughter 37
tender cuts 38
turkey 36
white meat 38
meringue
  copper bowl 92
milk 2, 3, 7, 9
  casein 9
  homogenization 3
  lactose 2, 4
  light 4
  low-fat 3
  milky way 9
  scalding 4, 5, 14
  skim 3
  whole 3
molasses 78
MSG 30, 75, 93, 94
mushrooms 30
  poisonous 31

N

nitrites 37

O

okra 26
olive 26, 27
  oil 26
  oleropein 27
onion 56
  Chicago 56
  laws 57
  sweet 56
  tears 56
  types 57

P

Pasturization 3
peanut 59
postum 69
potato 1
pumpkin 24

R

rennet 9
rhubarb 23
rice
  arborio 63
  aromatic 63
  christmas 63
  history 61
  long grain 63
  milled 62
  types 62
  vinegar 64
  wild 62
rye 61

S

salt 7, 95
  color 96
  iodine 96
  kosher 96
  salary 96
  sea 96
  sour 97
sausage 41
  botulism 42
  making 42
  origination 41
  uncooked 42
shallot 58
sorghum 80

spice
  anise 45
  basil 44
  caraway 45
  coriander 45
  cumin 45
  fennel 45
  majoram 44
  oregano 44
  parsely 46
  pepper 46
  peppermint 44
  rosemary 45
  sage 45
  thyme 45
starch 32, 95
  arrowroot 95
  potato 95
  root 95
succotash 65
suet 41
sugar 77
  beets 79
  brown 79
  caramelizing 97
  raw 77
  turbinado 79
  white 78

T

tapioca 95
taste (sense of) 93
tea
  caffeine 50
  iced 49
  legend 49
  varieties 49
three sisters 66

tomato 25
truffles 30
tubers 1

V

vanilla 97
vegetable 21
  brussel sprout 23
  cabbage 23
  carrot 21
  eggplant 24
  peppers 24
  potato 21, 22
  radish 21
  sweet potato 22
  yam 22
vinegar 7, 41, 58, 99
vitamin 86

W

wheat 60
  flour 60
wine 70, 71
  cork 73

Y

yam 1
yeast 33
  proof 33
yogurt 13

About the Author

Mike Bellino has an eclectic background in music, sound recording, aerospace, micro farming and electrical engineering. But at the end of the day, it all comes down to cooking and creating a meal for his family to enjoy together. Since he made his first "Wacky Cake" as a youth, he's been captivated by cooking and its inner workings. The desire to "know how things work" has motivated him to read, learn, try, endure failures and even occasionally succeed.

Mike makes his home with his wife, Mary, and five children on 23 acres in Bradford, New Hampshire. During the day, Mike is a mild-mannered electrical engineer. On weekends and evenings, to stave off boredom, he and his family raise chickens, turkeys, hogs, grow vegetables, tap maple trees, harvest wild blackberries and keep bees for their Circle Bell micro-farm.

About the Illustrator

Christopher Bellino, eldest son of the Author, hand drew the illustrations using soft pencil on bristol board. Chris was 15 years-old at the time these illustrations were drawn.

Printed in Great Britain
by Amazon